Foreword

"**RUN TO THE FLOOR FOR COUNTRY WESTERN ... LINE DANCING**" is truly the most comprehensive and complete line dance instructional manual that I have seen anywhere in my nine years of country dancing experience. The extensive, yet easy to follow guidance in Hilton's new book gives beginning as well as experienced country western dancers a solid advantage in country line dancing.

To say the book is complete is an understatement. There isn't anything about line dancing, dance floor etiquette, music, dancer attire, or dance guidance that you won't find between the covers of the book.

Hilton and I have been associates in business and in dancing for the past three years. He has brought his engineering expertise and gregarious nature to bear in preparing this well organized, complete, and truly outstanding new dance manual.

As Founder and President of the World Champion Wild Rose Dancers and a Silver Division Couples Competitor, I am pleased to offer my congratulations to Hilton on this major project.

To dancers everywhere! This book will bring you hours of enjoyment and most assuredly enhance your dancing skills.

Good Dancing,
　　Dick Fanus
　　　　Founder & President,
　　　　The 1993-1994 World Champion Wild Rose Dancers

Preface

RUN TO THE FLOOR FOR COUNTRY WESTERN ... LINE DANCING was written to help both beginners and advanced country western dancers enjoy this ever-expanding and popular art form. Two years ago, you would have had trouble finding country western dance instructions. Today, you can find instruction any night of the week. In fact, a country western saloon would be remiss in its responsibilities if it did not offer dance lessons at least one night per week. Now, the problem is finding a place to take lessons where there is room to get onto the dance floor.

RUN TO THE FLOOR FOR COUNTRY WESTERN ... LINE DANCING is organized into ten chapters. The first two chapters — Basics ... or Getting Started and Learning To Line Dance introduce the fundamentals of country western dancing: dance floor etiquette, dancing hints, the beat — adding music, cue sheets, and basic line dancing steps. After learning a few of the basics, you'll feel comfortable about proceeding further.

Chapters 3 through 9 detail many of the more popular line dances, with easy to follow instructions. The written instructions are supported by user-friendly illustrations (over four hundred). This unique feature of RUN TO THE FLOOR FOR COUNTRY WESTERN ... LINE DANCING will help you understand and learn country western dancing easier and quicker. This type of consolidated country western dancing information couldn't be found in any one source until now.

Chapter 10 — Music provides a unique list of all types of country western dances with some of the more popular songs to which the dances are performed.

RUN TO THE FLOOR FOR COUNTRY WESTERN ... LINE DANCING was designed and written to aid the person wanting to learn and participate in this dynamic, living art form. When learning to dance, you will want to use all the tools available. Currently, the available tools are public lessons, private lessons, dance videos, cue-sheets (someone's personal notes), flash cards, and a very few, hard-to-find books. RUN TO THE FLOOR FOR COUNTRY WESTERN ... LINE DANCING was written to fill that void.

The book is written to help you learn country western line dancing so you can "RUN TO THE FLOOR" to have fun and party hard.

Hilton Osborne's

RUN TO THE FLOOR FOR COUNTRY WESTERN ...

LINE DANCING

Including such features as:

47 Popular Line Dances

Easy Step by Step Moves

Over 400 User-friendly Illustrations

Dancing Hints

Key Foot Patterns

Suggested Dance Music

Etiquette

Griffin Publishing
Glendale, California

10   9   8   7   6   5   4   3   2   1

ISBN 1-882180-37-2

Griffin Publishing
544 Colorado Street
Glendale, California 91204

Telephone: 1-800-423-5789

Manufactured in the United States of America

Table of Contents

Chapter 6 — Intermediate Line Dances

Chapter 7 — Expert Line Dances

Chapter 8 — Advanced Expert Line Dances

Chapter 9 — Circle Line Dances

Chapter 10 — Music

Addendum

Dances-At-A-Glance

From the Author

After hundreds and hundreds of pleasurable hours of research (dancing and dance lessons) and a few frustrations RUN TO THE FLOOR FOR COUNTRY WESTERN ... LINE DANCING became real. I hope this book increases your dancing enjoyment.

You may find that a line dance is performed differently in different dancing establishments or other than as detailed in these pages. Please don't allow that to detract from your enjoyment. One of the fascinations of line dancing is that it is a group activity. Join the group! What you have learned here should help if any adjustments are necessary.

A super special thanks to all of my friends who have aided in the realization of this project. These include the numerous instructors whose years of instruction have found their concepts and ideas in these pages. Pattsy Phillips and Richard Brown are a few of the many competent and knowledgeable instructors who have reviewed the manuscript. Judy Keir, Vivian Eaton, and Karen Thoroughman labored for countless hours hunting for errors and inconsistencies Your labors are appreciated.

It was Dick Fanus who gave me the idea to build on his earlier book. His kind words in the Forward are greatly appreciated.

Kenneth Osborne was the brother who was always available in the late hours of the evening for consultation. It was Ken's insistence that provided the impetus to add the user-friendly illustration to the test. Most of all, I'm grateful to my wife, Ann Haws Osborne, whose support, creativity, encouragements, and journalistic skills made this work a quality work for your enjoyment.

Your comments are appreciated — so send a note.
THANK YOU!

Chapter 1
Basics—Getting Started

Introduction

Entering the world of $70 brightly-colored western shirts, $50 silver shirt collar tips, $175 white lacy dresses, $100 to $1,500 boots made from exotic animal skins, $5,000 gold Rolex watches, $200 silver and gold belt buckles, $250 black Stetson hats, $100 feathered hat bands, $110 stone-washed designer jeans, and $60 tooled leather belts can be intimidating!

After watching my first dance lesson, I left the dance hall thoroughly intimidated. And not just because of the pricey gear. On and on I grumbled: "Those people are not learning how to dance. They know how to dance. They're professionals!" So I thought. With some encouragement from a friend, a return trip was undertaken ... reluctantly.

Those return trips now number into the hundreds. After learning a few line dances, the real challenge was in remembering them. That challenge soon led to a second opportunity: Writing dance instructions for others that are easy to read, easy to follow, and really teach you how to dance.

Country Western Line Dancing is one of the fastest growing forms of dancing. Why do several hundred folks of all ages crowd onto a small dance floor for line dancing? Why do some of those enthusiastic dancers drive hours to join the crowd on the floor?

Hopefully, this book will help you understand the answers to those questions, and lead you to all the fun of country western dancing — especially line dancing.

The Line Dance

Just what is a line dance? It is a group or sequence of repeatable, choreographed steps or body movements performed to music by any number of individuals, usually standing in straight lines facing one particular direction (referred to as a wall).

After the first sequence of body movements has been performed, the dancer usually changes direction (wall) and repeats the sequence of movements while facing a different wall. Another form of line dancing is the circle or round dance; which is a form of line dancing performed in a circle. The circle dance fits the definition of a line dance when you consider a circle as a continuous line.

Line dances have many fascinating features. Usually, they are performed to popular country western music. The dancers generally are not paired. You might find 27 men and five women on the floor at any one time, or vice versa.

For some reason, country western dancers resent having their art form referred to as square dancing. So what is the difference between the two types of dancing? Dances, such as the 10-STEP, FUNKY COWBOY, COWBOY CHA-CHA, TEXAS 2-STEP, 2-STEP, waltzes, belt polishing dances and SQUARE DANCING, are just different types of country western dancing.

However, SQUARE DANCING has many basic differences from the other types of country western dancing. First, SQUARE DANCING is directed by a dance caller. The caller is a person who tells the dancers which dance movements to perform and when to execute them. The other forms of country western dancing have no caller. Secondly, SQUARE DANCING is for couples.

Both types of dancing are very structured forms of country western dancing. The amount of creativity and variety you see added to even the very structured line dances is surprising.

Today's country western dancing is a combination of jazz, rap, square dancing, clogging, ballroom dancing, swing, rock and roll, and just pure country. It's today! It's now! It's hot! And it's ever so popular because it's fun.

Some of the basic forms of country western dancing include: couples dances (2-STEP, WALTZ, CHA-CHA, EAST COAST SWING, WEST COAST SWING, POLKA, belt polishing dances ...), couples mixer dances (THE BARN DANCE ...), line dances (ACHY BREAKY, THE TUSH PUSH, COWBOY BOOGIE, TAHOE TWIST, FLYING 8 ...), and circle dances (TRAVELING FOUR CORNERS, ROULETTE WHEEL ...). The 2-STEP and line dances are the most popular forms of country western dancing.

How many different line dances exist? The easier question is: "How many different versions of HONKY TONK WALKIN' are there?" New line dances are being choreographed every day, so the number of dances changes all the time. I would estimate the number at well over seven hundred by the summer of 1994.

Practice ... Practice ... Practice

What is the secret to learning country western dancing?

Practice! Practice! Have fun practicing!

And have more fun dancing.

If there is a secret to learning country western line dancing, it is repetition. The more you practice, the more quickly you will become a proficient dancer. The more you know about dancing, the easier it becomes.

Line dances offer the single individual an opportunity to practice without a partner for couples dances. So, be encouraged to learn some line dances. In addition, line dancing teaches the basics for couples dancing — even without a partner.

Community dances, public saloons, honky-tonks, dance clubs, private events and country western saloons are just a few of the best places to learn. A friend's house or apartment is a good place to practice.

But, how do you remember a new dance when practicing at home or with a friend? Dance videos are expensive. They cover only a few dances per tape, and take lots of time to watch. Cue sheets are hard to find, and they sometimes are poorly written and difficult to understand. This book should help refresh your memory when you have trouble remembering a difficult series of steps or patterns.

The purpose of this book is to help you learn country western line dancing so that you can run to the floor ... and join in all the fun.

Why Line Dancing?

Why is line dancing so popular? Why do folks from all walks of life drive hours to pay for country western dance lessons and to dance? Good questions! And there are good answers:

1. **Line dancing is just pure, simple, unadulterated fun.** After watching a group of line dancers do their stuff for a few moments, you *know* they're having fun because they *are* having fun. And you'll want to RUN TO THE FLOOR to join them.

2. **You don't have to have a partner for line dancing.**

3. **Line dancing will provide you with great personal satisfaction** from your accomplishments.

4. **Line dancing is good physical exercise** — a low-impact aerobic workout. A few minutes of dancing the WILD WILD WEST will raise anyone's pulse rate.

5. **Line dancing, like any form of dancing, allows you to express joy and happiness.**

6. **Line dancing teaches coordination.** If you have two left feet, learning a few line dances will eliminate one of them.

7. **Line dancing teaches rhythm.** It will help you improve or develop your feel for rhythm.

8. **Line dancing will build your self-confidence and self-esteem.**

9. **Line dancing teaches you dance turns,** so when you dance with a partner, the turns are second nature.

10. **Line dancing allows dancers an opportunity to show-off** without being exhibitionists. When you line dance, it is acceptable to strut your stuff — show your plumage.

11. **Line dancing will introduce you to many wonderful people.** Line dancers are friendly folks. In fact, some of the greatest people in the world are country western dancers. Most generally, country western dancers just love to dance.

12. **Line dancing forces you to learn the difference between left and right.** Would you believe that?

13. **Line dancers like to hug each other.** If you could use an occasional,

friendly, old-fashioned hug, then country western dancers are for you.

14. **Line dancing will improve your posture.**

15. **Line dancing reminds you how to count.** As strange as it may seem, one does need to know how to count.

16. **Line dancing will improve timing.** You will learn to walk and move with grace and style.

17. **Line dancing improves your precision** with its many challenging dance steps.

18. **Line dancing teaches you etiquette**, both on and off the dance floor.

19. **Line dancing teaches you to respect the rights of others.**

20. **Line dancing teaches you to appreciate the efforts of others.**

21. **Line dancing allows you to dress in a different attire and relax in a different environment.** Perhaps this is just what is needed after a hard day of work; an opportunity to escape to a different world for a few hours.

22. **Line dancing improves your powers of concentration.** Not only do you get physical exercise from line dancing, but it requires a fair amount of mental exercise and concentration.

23. **Line dancing allows a tremendous amount of self-expression and creativity**, even with its structured surroundings.

24. **Line dancing is wonderful to watch.** It is perfectly acceptable to watch line dancers doing THE TUSH PUSH. It is especially enjoyable watching a TUSH PUSH contest. And that's the truth!

25. **Line dancing teaches steps for couples dancing.** Many of the dance steps that you would do with a partner are found in line dances. For example, the waltz and the Cha-Cha are just two of the steps that you also could do with a partner.

26. **Line dancing, like any form of dancing, provides an outlet from daily pressures.**

Truly, line dancing complies with all federal and state regulations in regard to discrimination. Line dancing does not discriminate for any reason: not for age, not for sex, not for education, not for race, not for financial status, not for physical appearance nor abilities, not for size, and not for mental capacities — although a *little* gray matter between your ears definitely is an asset.

What To Wear

Half the fun of country western dancing is the clothing — boots, shirts, hats, dresses ... and the list goes on. The more you dance, the more crowded your closet will become with western wear. Perhaps without realizing it, you already have a good start on a country western wardrobe. Most of us already have clothes that we wear to county fairs and similar events. These will work fine for starters. You'll probably find, too, that your first pair of boots will grow to several pairs faster than a field of corn on the 4th of July.

As in most situations, there is an appropriate time and place for everything. So what do you wear and when? You would not want to appear in a dance competition wearing a T-shirt, nor would you want to wear your best lacy dress to a Saturday morning dance lesson. As for Saturday night at your local dance saloon or dance hall, almost anything goes. You will find everything from wild T-shirts and cut-off jeans to shirts promoted by the popular performing artists and jeans promoted by rodeo heroes. Many stores specialize in western wear. If you cannot find the styles and sizes in a store, try shopping from one of the catalogs that specialize in western wear, such as *Sheplers* of Wichita, Kansas. For couples, matching shirts and jeans are the ticket. The styles and colors add fun and excitement to the dancing. Oh yes, don't forget the scents and fragrances for both the ladies and gentlemen.

The Feet

In football, it's "The knees, the knees, the knees;" with dancing, it's "The feet, the feet, the feet." The feet are the "beasts of burden" and with a little care they shouldn't cause you pain. The suggested foot wear is boots or shoes with leather soles. The foot wear should fit comfortably. Dancing requires that the feet slide and glide across the floor. Leather does the job very well.

Tennis shoes are definitely not recommended for dancing. Tennis shoes are designed to grip the floor, and it's a job they do extremely well. While dancing, gripping the floor is one thing you do not want your feet doing. At the other end of the scale, plastic soled shoes are too slick. Thus, leather-soled boots have a double bonus of being both stylish and functional.

The Boot

Today, cowboy boots are a country western fashion statement. For the cowboys of yesterday, the unique footwear functioned as protection against saddle chafing, rattlesnakes, barbed wire, briers and brambles, mesquite thorns, brush, and the weather. The pointed toe helps the cowboy find the stirrup when mounting his horse. The cowboy can touch his toe to the horse's side to give turning instructions.

The high, underslung heel adds to the cowboy's safety. Underslung describes the angle of the back of the heel. This type of heel keeps the cowboy's foot from slipping through the stirrup as he works, perched upon an unsteady mount. The heel also allows the cowboy to dig his heels into solid ground as he dismounts his horse.

The rows upon rows of fancy stitching on the shaft (the upper portion of the boot) have a practical function. The stitching reinforces the shaft, keeping it stiff and from sagging down the leg.

Buying Boots and the Fit

When purchasing your first pair of boots, I would suggest buying a rather inexpensive pair. In fact, I would suggest that you purchase several pairs of boots before you spend the big bucks for that special pair. Having several pairs of boots will give you a feel for what you like and for what feels comfortable on your feet. The variation in styles will complement your wardrobe. Plus, if you do not like the boots or they do not fit perfectly, you will have not lost much.

As for fit, if the boot does not feel really comfortable after the first five seconds that you have it on, it never will. A boot should fit and feel comfortable the first time you put it on. You should not experience any discomfort or pain whatsoever. There are just too many boots on the market to have a pair that is not comfortable.

Slip your foot into the boot while seated, then stand up to set the foot and seat the heel. Your heel will slip slightly in the heel of the boot. As you walk, the heel must have room to ride up a bit. The instep should be firm and provide support for the foot. The ball of the foot should fit right over the ball of the sole of the boot. Your toes will need ample space. Your toes should not feel like they are at the end of the boot, even with its pointed toes.

With a perfect fit, you will be able to wear the boots all day and night, never thinking about them unless you look down or someone complements you on their fine leather work. It is interesting that most folks think that their feet flatten, widen and shrink as the years accumulate. Bootmakers know that your feet grow slightly longer and narrower with age. Thus, it is wiser to buy boots slightly larger, rather than smaller, than required. You can accommodate larger boots for a perfect fit by wearing thicker socks, two pairs of socks, or a sole cushion liner for the boot. For that pair of tight-fitting boots, a little baby powder, foot powder or talcum powder can work minor miracles.

Country Western Dance Etiquette

Several courtesies, when observed and followed, will increase your enjoyment of country western dancing. Dance floor etiquette allows more people on the dance floor and it applies to all types of dancing — especially so, however, to line dancing. If there were just one rule of etiquette, it would be: *Have fun*! Respecting the rights of others will increase your level of dancing enjoyment ... and your fun.

Having taken several hundred dance lessons, I firmly believe that the need for dance floor etiquette cannot be overemphasized. Unfortunately, it doesn't take too long until you see every one of these niceties violated, resulting in loss of enjoyment for yourself and others.

Can you picture someone on the dance floor with a cigarette burning a hole in your new shirt or dress? Or, imagine a guy with a Tootsie Roll Pop in his mouth dancing cheek-to-cheek? Unfortunately, such lapses in common courtesies occur every evening on some dance floor somewhere. Please don't let that violator be you.

You will enjoy your dance time to its fullest by observing a few simple rules of dance floor etiquette.

General Dance Floor Etiquette

1. *Have fun and respect the rights of others to have fun.*
2. Smoke only in designated areas; never on the dance floor.
3. Never eat or drink on the dance floor.
4. If you knock over someone's drink, promptly and graciously replace it.

5. Couples should never move between line dancers. A pile-up may occur and needless injuries could be the result.

6. If you bump into someone, apologize — regardless of fault.

Figure 1

Dance Floor Etiquette
The Dance Floor
STAGE - BAND

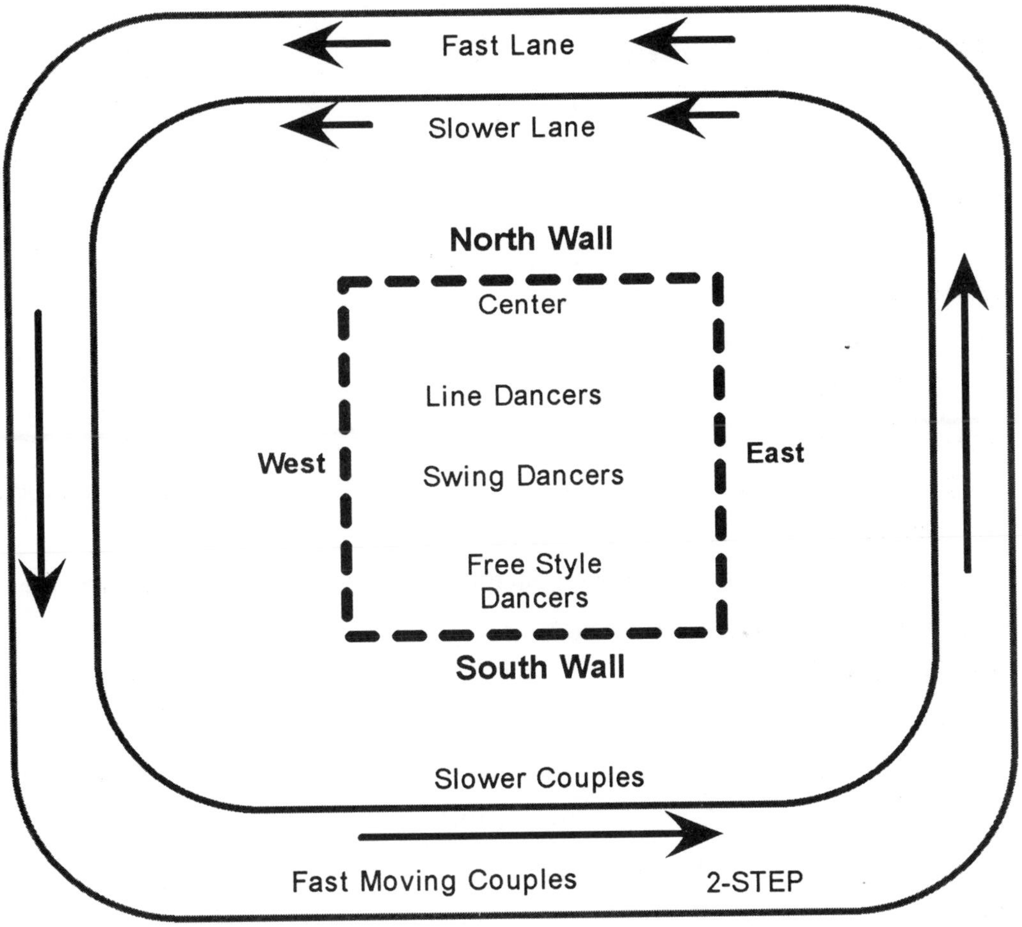

Line of Dance (LOD) is Counterclockwise

Fast Lane - Outside (Couples Progressive, 2-STEP, WALTZ, COWBOY POLKA, COWBOY CHA-CHA)
Slower Lane - Inside (Slower Dancing Couples)
Center Area - Center (Line dances. Slow couples, Swing Dancers, Rhythm 2-STEP, Free Style, CHA-CHA)

7.   Dance in the proper area of the dance floor. *(See Figure 1)*

8.   Remember: Excessive drinking and dancing, like driving, don't mix.

9.   Take care not to step on the feet of others, especially when stepping backward. A 210-pound man's size 14 boot can really damage a foot in a size 7 narrow shoe.

10. Free hands should be kept at the waist area to prevent getting hit by the swinging arms of others. Or vice versa.

11. Keep moving when you're in the fast (outside) lane. Conversations and dance lessons should be given in the center of the floor or off the dance floor.

12. Line of dance is counterclockwise as one looks down onto the floor.

13. Couples dance (2-STEP, POLKA, WALTZ, etc.) in the outside (fast) lane.

14. Those performing line dances, swing dances, rock-n-roll, and belt polishing dances use the center (slow) area.

15. Share your knowledge of dancing etiquette with others in a tactful, friendly manner.

16. Don't stand or suddenly stop in the fast lane.

17. Line dancers must give couples a few feet clearance on the edges of the floor.

18. Follow the leaders on the dance floor. You do not want to be the one going in the opposite direction.

Etiquette for Couples

Line dancing is an individual, performance art form. You would have trouble classifying the 10-STEP as a true line dance if you used the individuality as a criteria. The 10-STEP can be performed solo or by a couple, threesome or a group. Thus, it would only be fair to include a few dance floor courtesies involving couples.

1.   **Gentleman's Fault Rule** — The gentleman leads on the dance floor; thus, if a mistake is made, it is the gentleman's fault. Gentlemen "lead," ladies "follow."

2. Treat your partner with the greatest respect by avoiding injuring him/her. Men should lead with finger tips, avoiding pulling and yanking.

3. Women should just apply firm pressure (not holding) to man's hands with her finger tips. Likewise a man should not hold a lady's hands or fingers—just apply firm pressure to maintain contact. Ladies should avoid digging their finger nails into their partner's hands. Trust me, it hurts.

4. Men: Remember that your legs are generally longer than those of the women, so take small steps. Be considerate.

5. Dance at your partner's ability. Attempt fancy turns and movements only with your partner's knowledge and approval. Doing otherwise may be confusing and/or frustrating.

6. Be considerate of the man's hands. Women should wear smoothly finished rings or no rings at all. The man will hold and turn his hands in yours. A beautiful diamond ring can really reduce his enjoyment of dancing.

7. When asking a lady to dance, a gentleman should ask the lady if she would like to dance and name the type of dance: "Would you like to WEST COAST SWING?", or "Michelle, would you please join me in the 10-STEP."

8. If you intend to try a fancy turn or flip, let your partner know, or practice first. You are not going to make points if you flip a lady and she falls.

Etiquette for Lessons

Etiquette is just as important while taking dance lessons as it is while dancing. Include these items below in your knowledge of dance floor etiquette.

1. Be on time to the lesson. When you are late, the instructor has to repeat items just for you. Being late also slows your learning. Perhaps it would be better to miss the lesson completely than to be late.

2. Listen to the instructor. It is difficult for you to learn to dance with your mouth open.

3. Ask questions of the instructor: not another dancer. Others in the class might be having trouble with the same instructions.

4.   Attempt to get into a class with others of similar dancing abilities. If you are an advanced dancer in a beginner's class, do not disrupt the class by doing advanced turns or moves. No matter what your dancing level, you always should be able to learn something from a class.

5.   If you are not taking the class, respect those who are participating by not making noise or otherwise interfering with the class.

6.   Follow instructions. Proceeding ahead of the instructor is disruptive to the class.

7.   Let the instructor do the teaching. If someone asks for your help, direct them to the instructor. Or, you could always give personalized instructions after class.

Etiquette for Business

The saloon, dance hall, honky-tonk, bar, and other establishments that you frequent are in business to make money. They deserve and need your respect, consideration, and financial support. For the good of country western dancing and your future enjoyment, support the establishment. Your reward for these courtesies will be in having a place to dance in the future.

1.   You should support the business by purchasing drinks.

2.   Be considerate of the establishments' employees. Tip the servers generously.

3.   Follow the rules of the establishment.

4.   Respect the property of the establishment.

Above all ... *Have Fun*!

Dancing Hints for Success

The more time you spend in your boots on the dance floor, the easier it will become for you to learn new line dances. This list of dancing hints should speed your learning process.

General Tips

1.   **Learn and practice dance floor etiquette**
       Your dancing enjoyment will be increased by respecting the privileges and rights of others.

2. **Practice and repetition**

    Practice — have fun!

    Repetition — have fun!!

3. **Important terms and concepts**

    Terms to Learn: *Close* — closed position; *Step, Touch, Vine* — grapevine right and grapevine left; *Shuffle Step* — triple step. It is important to know the difference.

4. **Position on the dance floor**

    When learning a line dance that covers lots of floor, you might feel more comfortable being at the end of a line or by the edge of the floor. If you make a wrong move in that position, you won't necessarily bump into others. If you feel fairly comfortable with a dance, position yourself in the middle of a group of dancers, so you have someone to watch no matter which wall you are facing.

5. **Crowded dance floors**

    Okay, the dance floor is crowded and you need more room. There are several ways to solve the problem. You will find fewer folks on the floor early or later in the evening. You might even try an off night of the week, say Sunday or Monday. You might try a less popular establishment. Many times, the floor is empty when the band goes to break. Or, try dancing at your place, a friend's home or even a public park with a radio — Just be considerate of others with your sound equipment.

6. **Foot protection**

    Ladies would be well advised to wear boots. Open-toe shoes provide little or no protection. As with horseback riding, there are two types of riders: those who have been thrown, and those who will be thrown. Unfortunately, someone, someday, sometime will step too close to your foot for your pleasure.

7. **Don't drink and dance**

    Okay, have one drink. When you are attempting to learn, however, a few drinks will add to the difficulty. It is interesting to watch a person who is having trouble learning to line dance. Generally, alcohol is interfering with their learning process. Suggestion: Request a beer with a glass of ice — then pour the beer over the ice. The extra water will help replenish your body fluids, while keeping your beer cold.

Stick to wine or beer instead of mixed drinks. With wine or beer, you have an idea of how much alcohol you are consuming. With mixed drinks, it is difficult to judge your alcohol consumption.

Technical Tips

1.   Small steps

For several reasons, take small steps. First, it is easier to keep your balance when your feet are directly under your center of gravity (body). Second, when you are attempting to dance fast, taking small steps means you don't have to move your feet so far; thus, you appear to be moving fast. Third, if you make a mistake, it is easier to recover. Fourth, it takes less work to take small steps. Fifth, it is less likely that you will bump into others when taking small steps.

2.   Body weight changes

Changes in the distribution of your body weight must be made during dancing. Body weight must be changed for a STEP. Most generally, you change body weight on the beat of music. Usually, your weight changes from one foot to the other. For example, while stepping left-right-left your body weight changes from the left foot to the right foot, then back to the left foot. Your body weight does not change on touches, nor on heel, toe, hop, scoot, jump or point.

3.   Recovery

Recovery is the art or skill of missing a step, turn or move, and then catching up with the others. One of the keys to line dancing is recovery. When you first run to the floor to join a line dance, the chances are really good that you will miss a few steps. If you get behind, don't try to catch up. When you do get behind, pause for a moment and pick up the dance from the next part you know. Recovery is a technique that everyone easily learns.

4.   Gracefulness

Improve the gracefulness of your style by looking forward; not down at your feet. Looking forward, with eyes straight ahead and your head upright, improves body posture. The body should be kept upright and straight from the hips upward. Your shoulders are kept level with the floor. This body structure adds grace and elegance to your dancing style. With any form of dancing, and especially line dances, considerable style can be added with hand movement. Watch some good dancers and add the hand and arm movements that please you and enhance your dance style.

5. **Styling**

The appearance that you exhibit while dancing is referred to as styling. Other than the basic steps in a line dance, any embellishments and expressions that you add comprise your individual dancing style. Fundamental to style are principles such as rhythm, posture, relaxation, body economy, and execution techniques. Styling is your opportunity to add your personality to a line dance. Express yourself in a pleasing and graceful manner.

6. **Geography**

With line dancing, geography is an important consideration. As the line dance progresses, you move to different spots on the floor, but once you begin the dance again, you should be in the same general position in which you started the dance. For example, after 4 walls of THE TUSH PUSH, you should be in the same geographical spot on the dance floor as you were when the dance began. That is the way line dances are choreographed.

7. **Warm-ups**

Many of the more advanced line dances are very aerobic. It is recommended that warm-up exercises be performed to stretch and loosen tight muscles.

Instruction Tips

1. **Lots of dance lessons**

   With dancing, more is better. The more dance lessons that you take, the faster you'll learn. It is interesting, but even after hundreds of dance lessons, you still can learn something new.

2. **Different teachers**

   Take lots of dance lessons from lots of different teachers. All instructors have techniques and movements that they enjoy teaching and stress. By selecting a variety of teachers, you will have a fuller spectrum upon which to build your dance style.

3. **Outstanding instructors**

   Instructors have different formats for teaching their classes. Some of the better instructors begin each class with a review of dances learned in past classes. These practice sessions are highly recommended, especially when the reviewed line dances come with brief lessons. These review lessons also allow you to warm up those tight muscles.

   Remember: The more repetition, the quicker you will learn. Four or five review dances at the beginning of each lesson are enough. The review dances also serve as warm ups and generate excitement for the newcomers.

4. **Instruction techniques**

   When evaluating a teacher, pay attention to the techniques used to give instructions. A really good, seasoned instructor will use phrases such as: "Face the north wall" or "Face the stage"; *not* "Face that way" or "Face that wall". A superior teacher will say: "Right foot steps right" or "Left foot kicks forwards"; *not* "See this" or "Watch me" or "Like this" or "Right here." A good instructor knows that it is very difficult for everyone to see all the details of instruction on a crowded dance floor so the moves are described in clear and concise terms. What you really are looking for is a teacher who is easy to learn from and who makes learning fun.

5. **Watch good dancers**

   Watching other dancers dance can help you learn. Make sure the person you are watching is a good dancer and knows the dance.

The Beat — Adding Music

Dancers are in lines on the floor, facing the stage. They wait. The band begins. From the stage, you hear the count "5 - 6 - 7 - 8". The line dance has begun and, hopefully, everyone has started on the correct foot, is going in the same direction, and is on the correct beat with the music.

Without going into great detail, it is important to understand a little about music — the **beat, tempo,** and **rhythm.** When listening to music, you probably tap your foot. While tapping your foot to the music, you are following the beat. You have discovered that the beat is the regularly recurring pulsation of the music.

For the musician, the beat is divided into two parts: the **downbeat** and the **upbeat.** The drummer, or the base guitar in country western music, usually carries the beat and that is the sound that you follow when you tap your foot. With 4/4 timing, the musician has four downbeats and four upbeats. For the dancer, dancing the 2-STEP — 4/4 timing, the odd counts are downbeats and the even counts are upbeats. Counts 1, 3, 5, and 7 are downbeats. Counts 2, 4, 6, & 8 are upbeats.

Music has tempo or speed. Tempo is the time between beats or the distance between beats, measured in time. Tempo is measured as beats per minute (BPM). George Jones' "Honky Tonk Myself to Death" has 86 BPM — it's a slow song; whereas, The Oak Ridge Boys' "Standing By The River" has 148 BPM — it's a fast song. "I'd Fall In Love Tonight" by Anne Murray is a waltz and it has a BPM of 100.

Line dancing offers training in tempo and rhythm. It won't be long before you hear a new song and know that it has the perfect beat for your favorite dance. The Table 1 below shows the typical tempo for some popular dances.

Rhythm refers to how the beats are accented. While tapping your foot to some music, you observe that all beats are the same (4/4 timing): 1 - 2 - 3 - 4, 1 - 2 - 3 - 4 or 1 - 2 - 3 - 4 - 5 - 6 - 7 - 8. Then, when you listen to a waltz, you notice a difference in the rhythm (3/4 timing): $1'$ - 2 - 3 - $4'$ - 5 - 6, $1'$ - 2 - 3 - $4'$ - 5 - 6. The beat on $1'$ and $4'$ are heavier; they are accented. These are the steps (beats) in the waltz that are longer (emphasized). Rhythm is produced by the grouping of pulsations or beats. Fundamentally, all rhythm falls into one of two classes: double (2-count) or triple (3-counts). The double (2-counts) has a strong beat followed by a weak beat.

Table 1

Typical Rhythms for Some Popular Dances

TYPE OF DANCE	BPM/TEMPO
2-STEP	180-216
10-STEP	172-196
BLACK VELVET	94
CHA-CHA	84-120
EAST COAST SWING	134-220
POLKA	120-150
TUSH PUSH	140-164
WALTZ	88-116
WEST COAST SWING	98-156

You would count it as:

1 - 2, 1 - 2, 1 ... *or* 1 - 2 - 3 - 4, 1 - 2 - 3 - 4...

The triple (3-count) has one strong beat followed by two weak beats. The waltz is two triples. You would count it as:

$1'$ - 2 - 3 - $4'$ - 5 - 6, $1'$ - 2 - 3 - $4'$ - 5 - 6 ...

Figures 2, and 3 show the relationship of counting with the movement of the feet for a normal walk, 2-STEP and cha-cha step. With these particular steps, the distance that a foot moves is related to the beat or time. The more time the foot has to move, the further it moves.

With the waltz, each step gets the same count or time, but the first and fourth steps are long steps. The second, third, fifth, and sixth steps (on beats 2, 3, 5, and 6) are short or small steps in relation to steps on beats 1 and 4. The steady, fundamental beat of the music represents the skeletal structure of the music. This is the primary rhythm.

Why is this stuff important? Because you move with the music. You move with the beat. For each beat or count, you generally take a step or move or do something!

Line dances help you learn to feel and move with the music. You do this by watching and moving with the other dancers. If you are having trouble with a particular dance, count the beats and/or steps. This is especially true with the 10-STEP, 2-STEP or WALTZ ACROSS TEXAS.

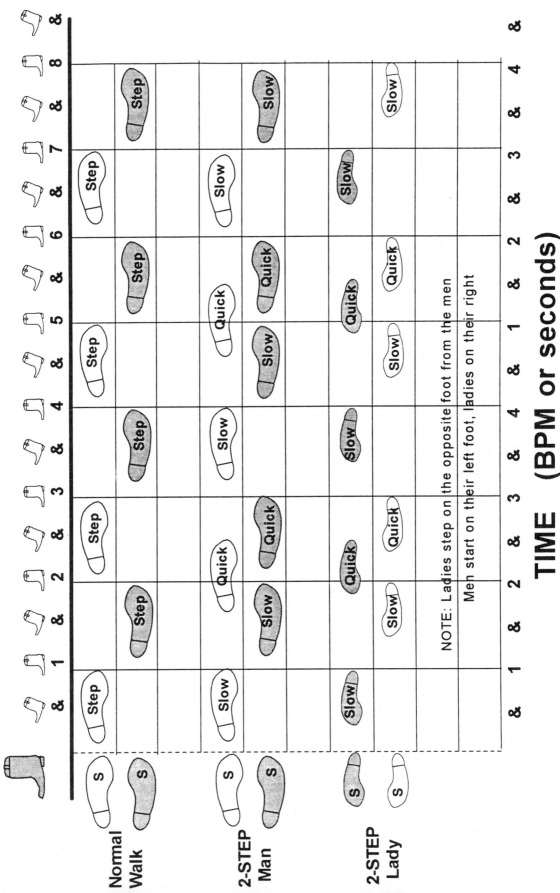

Figure 2

For each down beat, you count one. Most line dances are based on a 4 count: 1 - 2 - 3 - 4. Waltzes are based on a 3 count: 1 - 2 - 3, *or* 1 - 2 - 3 - 4 - 5 - 6.

Line dancing will help you develop or enhance your feel for rhythm and tempo. Feeling the rhythm and tempo will allow you to determine which dance to perform to a particular song. Before you know it, you'll easily recognize waltz, cha-cha, polka, swing and all the other rhythms within seconds of a song's beginning.

Figure 3

Counting For CHA-CHA & TRI-PLE STEP

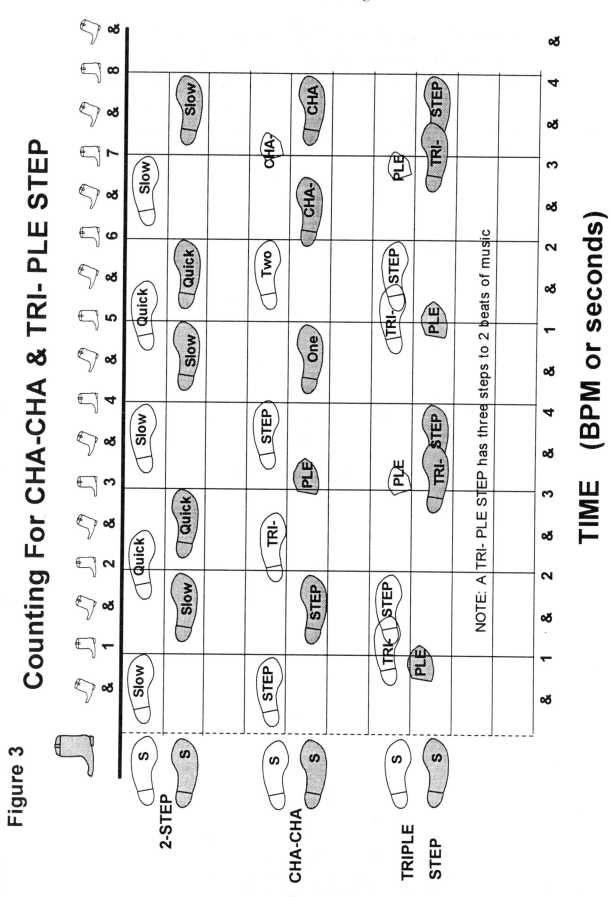

NOTE: A TRI-PLE STEP has three steps to 2 beats of music

TIME (BPM or seconds)

Figure 4

Counting For The Waltz

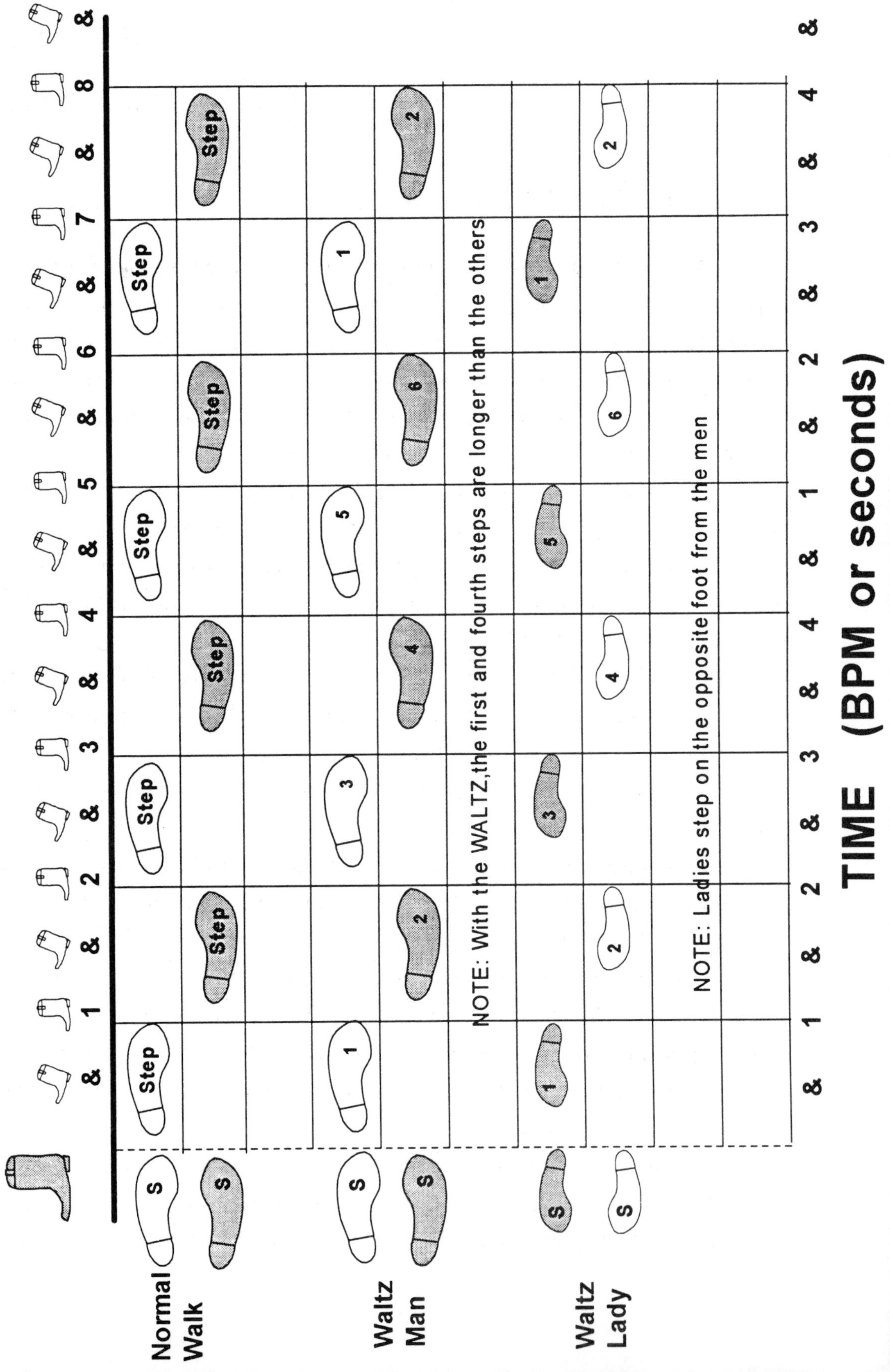
& 1 & 2 & 3 & 4 & 5 & 6 & 7 & 8 &
Normal Walk
Waltz Man
Waltz Lady
S
Step
NOTE: With the WALTZ, the first and fourth steps are longer than the others
NOTE: Ladies step on the opposite foot from the men
& 1 & 2 & 3 & 4 & 1 & 2 & 3 & 4 &
TIME (BPM or seconds)

Chapter 2
Learning To Line Dance

Learning Line Dances

What is the best way to learn Country Western Line Dancing? Start with the popular, easy dances — the ELECTRIC SLIDE, COWBOY BOOGIE. But, before you get excited and start dancing, it will help your learning progress if you understand a few basics. Body weight changes — shifting from foot to foot. When you dance, your weight changes from one foot to the other. At times you move a foot, but your weight does not change. Most instructors refer to a *STEP as a foot movement in which the body weight changes. A TOUCH is a foot movement in which weight does not change.* Most generally, a STEP and a TOUCH are executed on the beat. As you learn more about dancing, you will appreciate the importance of knowing the foot upon which your weight is resting. It is impossible to move a foot upon which your weight is resting, except to hop or scoot.

To begin, read through the section in this book entitled "Basic Line Dancing Steps" to become familiar with basic foot patterns and movements. Become familiar with the symbols (foot prints) used in the user-friendly illustrations. Hopefully the symbols are self-explanatory. *The right foot is always shaded, while the left foot is not shaded.*

Then, turn to the section on the specific dance in which you are interested. Read the directions for one block of steps, look at the illustrated foot prints, and slowly dance through the pattern. Repeat the block of steps several times.

Once you feel comfortable with that block, move to the next block. After doing eight to twelve steps, select a slow song and do the dance to the beat of the song. Repeat the process until the end of the dance. As soon as you feel confident about executing the steps to a beat, begin practicing the dance with the music/songs to which it is most often performed.

Practice, repetition, practice, repetition, and more practice is the real key to becoming a proficient dancer. Work for a while on one line dance until you feel comfortable with it. Then, add another ... and another, until you have a full repertoire.

Remember: Don't be overly concerned about the exact position of your feet. Follow the flow of the other dancers. Use foot positions that are comfortable to you and that fit the general flow of the dance.

Guide to Learning

Learning Country Western Line Dances is no different than learning anything else. You must take advantage of all the tools available: public and private dance lessons, help from friends, watching other dancers, videos, flash cards ... and this book. By using **RUN TO THE FLOOR FOR COUNTRY WESTERN ... LINE DANCING** as your at-home instructor, you should be able to considerably reduce the time that it otherwise would take you to learn the dances.

Public and private lessons from accomplished teachers help tremendously in the learning process. After a lesson, be sure to practice the dance whenever you can — even while waiting in line at the supermarket or while on a work break. A friend of mine listens to the radio at work and, when business is slow, practices the dances. You can even sit at your desk and unobtrusively practice your foot movements. The point is, after you learn a line dance, practice it.

Dancin' to Different Drummers

Most of us would like to be able to go onto the dance floor and find everyone doing each line dance exactly the way that we do them. That would be standardization and it "ain't gonna" happen.

The BOOT SCOOTIN' BOOGIE performed in California's Antelope Valley is completely different from the BOOT SCOOTIN' BOOGIE done in Fresno, in the state's central valley. You just have to learn to adjust to the many different styles, steps and patterns.

In the spring of 1993, Dolly Parton released the song "Romeo." At last count, there were six different versions to the line dance ROMEO. The HONKY TONK WALKIN' done to the Kentucky Headhunters' "Honky Tonk Walkin'" has ***seven*** versions. The manager of that band even had a contest to determine the version they liked best.

Which version of a line dance do you want to learn? Your best bet is to become proficient in the dances performed locally. Then, it's a fairly simple matter to readjust your steps when necessary.

If you dance two or more nights per week, or teach others to dance, it's easy to remember all the different dances and versions of dances. If you don't dance regularly, then it becomes a little more difficult.

Once you have learned the basics of line dancing, you quickly can learn an entirely, new dance or make adjustments to a more familiar routine by watching others.

An accomplished country western dancer can travel anywhere, watch the dancers for a short period of time, and be able to join in on the fun. Even if you don't know the dance, get out on the floor — perhaps out of the way — and attempt to follow along.

After a few walls, you will have learned the flow of the dance.

Remember: For a country western line dancer, the most important rules are:

— Learn the basics

> **— Follow dance floor etiquette**
>> **— Be patient with yourself**
>>> **(we all learn at different rates)**
>>> **— Have fun!**

Using Line Dancing Cue Sheets

In compiling this book, every attempt has been made to provide handy, user-friendly cue sheets for both the beginner and the boot-worn dancer. For the beginner, illustrations along with detailed descriptions of foot movements will be a great aid in learning country western line dancing. For the more advanced dancer, a brief description is provided as a refresher.

Each cue-sheet starts with the name of the dance in capital letters. The difficulty of each dance is listed: very easy, easy, moderate, intermediate, expert, and advanced expert. It is suggested that you learn the easy dances first.

Next, you will find the type of dance with the number of walls. What does "wall" mean? It is the direction that you face while doing a line dance. The stage is considered the first wall. Line dances are either 1-, 2-, or 4-wall dances. The number of walls refers to the number of different walls with which the dance sequences begin. The back, right side and left side are considered the walls.

The illustrations refer to the walls as N (north), S (south), E (east), and W (west). When working through the steps with the illustrations, it might be helpful to face north, holding the illustration in front.

Also included in each cue sheet, you'll find the number of counts for the dance. It is possible for a line dance to have 78 steps (beats/counts) and, in reality, only have 76 movements. Or the dance could have 76 steps and have 78 movements. Such is the case with the BOOT SCOOTIN' BOOGIE. The pause is considered a count, but no movement is required.

Music appropriate for each dance is listed. At the end of the book you will find a complete list of dances along with suggested dance music.

The actual dance instructions are divided into small workable sections — usually 4 to 8 counts. Each section begins with abbreviated instructions for the advanced dancer.

Following the abbreviated instructions, you'll find detailed instructions for the beginning line dancer. The first number refers to the count sequence in the dance. The second number refers to the count. The second number will be used to help you stay in step *(See the cue sheet)*.

Following the user-friendly illustrations makes these instructions super easy to learn. The right foot, heel and toe (sole) are always shaded. The left foot is not shaded. The "S" on the foot indicates the starting position for that pattern. The numbers on the feet represent the sequence count.

The instructions should be followed until the end. Then, the sequence of instructions is repeated until the end of the song. The number and type of turns in a line dance will determine the number of walls.

Where necessary, *"Notes"* have been added to emphasize special points. For example, the popular ELECTRIC SLIDE is a very simple, repetitive line dance. After performing the dance a few times, you'll want to add embellishments. Some of these embellishments are found in the *"Notes."*

Illustrations: Please realize that the illustrations are a guide to foot placement. You should adjust your foot placement to your dance style and to what is comfortable to you.

Also, for some illustrations, foot placement has been changed slightly to aid in clarification. For example, whenever a foot steps in the same place, each count is shown on the foot. What happens when the foot is almost in the same place? The illustration will usually show the foot not overlapping, but beside the other foot.

Note: TRI -PLE STEP illustrations — Illustrating the triple step created a dilemma. Your body weight changes on each of the three steps. The second step of a triple step is usually done on the ball of the foot — you don't have time to place the whole foot down. The illustration should show a whole foot. The TRI -PLE STEP illustration shows two full feet with an opposite toe because it makes a better representation of your foot action, makes for a more unique graphic, and makes a more recognizable illustration.

Line Dancing Cue Sheet

DANCE NAME

Type of dance; dance difficulty — very easy, easy, moderate, intermediate, expert, and advanced expert; number of walls — number of counts

Music: Suggested song by performing artist

Description: information concerning the dance

ABBREVIATED DESCRIPTION OF MOVES (1-4 Counts)

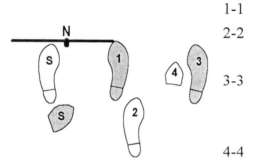

1-1	Detailed description of move
2-2	The first number is the sequence count for the dance
3-3	The second number is the count number of this particular group pattern
4-4	Left toe touches by right foot

Grapevine Right (5-8 Counts)

5-1	Right foot steps to right side
6-2	Left foot steps behind right foot
7-3	Right foot steps right
8-4	Left foot touches by right heel

END OF DANCE — Repeat patterns until end of song or TTTD (Too Tired To Dance).

Notes: Any special instructions or interesting information concerning the dance is entered here.

Basic Line Dancing Steps — *Key Foot Patterns*

Many of the steps or patterns that you encounter with line dances are repeated over and over. As a result, once a few basic steps are learned, it is very simple to put them together in different arrangements for different dances. Some of the newer dances will have some unique moves that add variety (embellishments) to the dance.

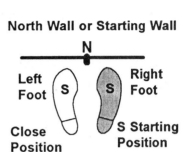

North Wall or Starting Wall

N

Left Foot

Right Foot

Close Position

S Starting Position

It is assumed that we all know words such as forward, back, right and left. It is always interesting however, to watch a beginning line dance class, as the instructor tells someone to use their "other" right foot. Believe me, we all have stepped left when wanting to step right. The first set of user-friendly illustrations are self-explanatory. The "S" on the feet signifies the starting position. The numbers are the counts from the starting position. These numbers also refer to the verbal description of the steps.

> **Note: It is very important for you to understand the difference between a STEP and a TOUCH as they relate to changes of your body weight while dancing. With a STEP, body weight is shifted to the stepping — moving foot. With a TOUCH, your body weight does not shift. It stays on the foot that did not move.**

Before you start your first line dance, there are a few words that will help you learn and understand dance movements: **step, touch, close, vine, and triple step**.

1. Step — A foot movement that results in a change in body weight. A *step* is illustrated by showing the complete foot – heel and sole.

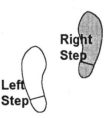

Right Step

Left Step

2. Touch — A *touch* is a foot movement that does not result in a change of body weight. The difference between a *step* and a *touch* is an important concept to remember. With a *touch*, the foot, heel, or toe will

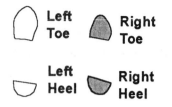

Left Toe Right Toe

Left Heel Right Heel

touch forward, back, or to the side. A *touch* is illustrated by showing that part of the foot which touches the dance floor — heel or sole.

3. Close — The *close position* or *close* is the standard starting position for a line dance. Both feet are placed together, comfortably under the center of the body. See the first illustration at the top of the previous page.

4. Vine — A *vine* is a very common series of side steps. Details follow under grapevine.

5. Triple Step — The *triple step* (Shuffle), shown as TRI- PLE STEP in the user friendly-illustrations, is a quick three (left - right - left *or* right - left - right) step pattern performed in two counts.

Right Triple Step

Several of the more common foot patterns found in line dances are detailed here as a collection. These patterns, choreographed with music, make up 90 percent of all line dances.

Moving Left Foot

Moving Right Foot

Ball Change and Kick Ball Change

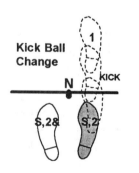

Kick Ball Change

The Ball Change is a step on the ball of one foot while quickly changing weight to the other foot. This usually is done as part of a Kick Ball Change. The Kick Ball Change is a form of Ball Change. For example, you would kick the right foot forward, bring the right foot back under the body and step on the right foot, changing weight to the left foot in a two count movement. The outlined foot illustrates a moving foot.

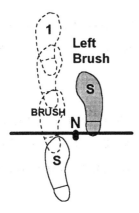

Brush

The Brush is accomplished when one moving foot touches or "kisses" the floor beside the foot supporting the body weight. The Brush is a sweeping motion.

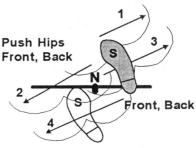

Bump Hips or Hip Bumps

This movement involves rocking the hips from one side to the other or left - right - left - and right. The hips are rocked by keeping one knee stiff, and bending the opposite knee.

Buttermilk

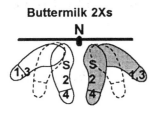

Lifting up on the balls of both feet spreading heels out to the side, then bringing the heels back together, is referred to as a Buttermilk (aka: butterfly, heel splits, splits, scissors, pigeon toes). Each Buttermilk takes two counts. In many line dances, the dancers call out the word "Buttermilk" while performing the step.

Charleston

A Charleston or Charleston step is a 3- or 4-count step pattern: step forward with left foot, kick forward with right foot, step back on right foot, and touch left foot behind. Usually, you clap when kicking forward. The Charleston also can be done with the left foot kicking forward.

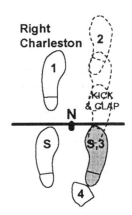

Close or Close Position

Feet are placed together comfortably under the body, pointing forward. Line dances usually begin in the Close position.

Cross

With a Cross (aka: Crossover), one foot is crossed in front of the other foot. Crossovers differ from grapevines or vines. With a grapevine, one foot is placed behind the other foot. With a Crossover, one foot is crossed in front of the other foot. In a Crossover left, you step with the right foot over the left. For a Crossover right, you step with the left foot over the right foot.

Duck Step

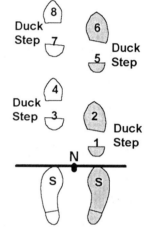

The Duck Step (aka: Duck Walk, Strut or Country Strut) is a two-count step in which the heel is touched to the floor first, and then the toe is rolled (lowered or slapped) to the floor. Usually, a dance will include a right duck walk, left duck walk, right duck walk, and left duck walk. Body weight changes on a Duck Step.

Fan

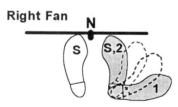

The Fan is a swing of the foot to the right or left, with the toe moving to the side and back while the heel remains on the floor. The heel is the pivot point.

Grapevine or Vine (Basic)

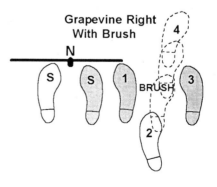

A Grapevine or Vine (aka: Grapevine Right, Grapevine Left, Vine Right, Vine Left) is a 3- or 4-count move. To perform the Grapevine, you step to the side with one foot, step behind that foot with the other foot, and then step to the side again with the first foot.

The last foot move (count) can be a stomp, brush, touch, step, or scoot. A turn can be done on the third or fourth count of the Grapevine. It is common practice to clap whenever you stomp.

Grapevine Right is performed by stepping right with the right foot, stepping behind the right foot with the left foot, stepping right with the right foot, and then touching the right foot with the left foot. You clap when your feet touch.

Grapevine Left, or Vine Left, is the opposite of a Grapevine Right. You step left with the left foot, step behind the left foot with the right foot, step left with the left foot, and then touch the left foot with the right foot. Again, you can clap when your feet touch.

Heel or Toe *(Also see Touch)*

The Heel and Toe are very similar moves. The Heel or Toe is touched to the floor in front, back or to the side. There is no change of body weight.

Heel Touches

Hips *(See Bump Hips)*

Hitch

A Hitch is performed by lifting the knee up, generally while scooting the other foot or hopping on the other foot.

Hook, Boot Hook

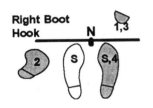

Right Boot Hook

The Hook (aka: Boot Hook, Right Hook, Left Hook, Right Boot Hook, Left Boot Hook) is a 4-count series of movements: heel touches forward, foot lifts to the opposite leg so that the calf touches the leg just below the knee, heel touches forward, close. The height to which the leg is lifted can vary depending upon how you want to accent the Boot Hook. The hook can be done with either foot. The funny looking foot represents how the foot looks as seen from above.

Hop

A Hop is a moving of the body forward, backward, or sideways without a change of body weight to the other foot. With a Hop, the foot leaves the floor. Usually, the opposite leg is raised with the knee bent, in a movement similar to a hitch.

Jazz Box

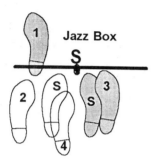

The Jazz Box is a 4-count move in which one foot is crossed over the other, you step back on the other foot, and then the first foot closes together. For example: you cross your right foot over the left foot, step back on the left foot, step right on the right foot, and left foot stomps by the right foot.

Point — Point Right and Point Left

A Point is a toe touch with no change of body weight. Pointing can be to the front, back, or side.

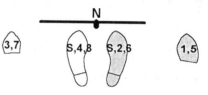

Rock or Rock Step

A Rock is a shifting of body weight from one foot to the other. The feet usually do not change position on the floor.

Scoot

A Scoot is a forward, side, or backward movement on one foot on the floor. Usually the opposite foot is lifted off the floor. With a Scoot, the scooting foot slides on the floor.

Star

A Star is a toe point to the front, side, and the rear (back) or vice versa. This is a 3-count move.

Step

With a Step (aka: Step Right, Step Left, Step Forward, Step Back), the foot is moved to the front, back or side with a change of body weight from the other foot, usually on the beat. With a touch, your weight does not change or shift.

Shuffle Step or Triple Step or Polka

The Shuffle or Triple Step (aka: Shuffle Step, Right Shuffle Step, Left Shuffle Step, Triple Step Right, Triple Step Left) is three quick steps performed in two counts (counted as 1 - and - 2). In a Left Forward Shuffle Step, you step forward on your left foot, step with your right toes to your left heel, and then step forward with your left foot. You can do a Shuffle Step toward the front, back, or side.

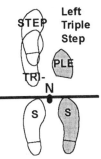

Stomp

A Stomp involves hitting the floor with the whole foot. One of the purposes of the stomp is to make noise. Be careful that you don't Stomp so hard that injury results. It is common practice to clap whenever you stomp.

Strut *(Also, see Duck Step)*

The Strut is a slow, 2-count, forward foot motion in which the heel is touched to the floor first, and then the ball of the foot is touched to the floor. Body weight changes on a Strut.

Swivel/Twist

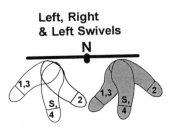

A Swivel is performed by turning on the balls of both feet with the heels going from one side or back to the center. A Twist is moving the heels from one side to the other. The illustration shows a left swivel, right twist, left twist, and a right swivel.

Triple Step *(See Shuffle Step)*

Touch

A Touch is when the foot touches the floor without a shift of body weight, usually on the beat. The Heel and Toe are very similar moves. Usually, a TOE or HEEL touches. Most often, the HEEL or TOE touches the floor in front, back or to the side.

Wall

A wall refers to the direction of a line dance. There are four walls. A line dance will either be a 1-, 2-, or 4-wall dance.

W West Wall

Vine *(See Grapevine)*

Chapter 3
Very Easy Line Dances

10-STEP or THE TEXAS POLKA

Circle dance, very easy, every dancer should know, couples or singles, one circle — 18 counts

Music: "Orange Blossom Special" by Johnny Cash, "The Fireman" by George Strait, "Eight Days a Week" by Lorrie Morgan, "Devil Went Down to Georgia" by The Charlie Daniels Band, "I Love a Rainy Night" by Eddie Rabbit

Description: Fast-moving dance — no matter where you go, the 10-STEP is done once or twice each evening. It is just a very popular dance and one of the first dances you'll want to learn.

This dance may be done by individuals, groups or couples. Couples dance in the sweetheart position, moving counter-clockwise in the outside lane. Individuals dance as a group or by themselves.

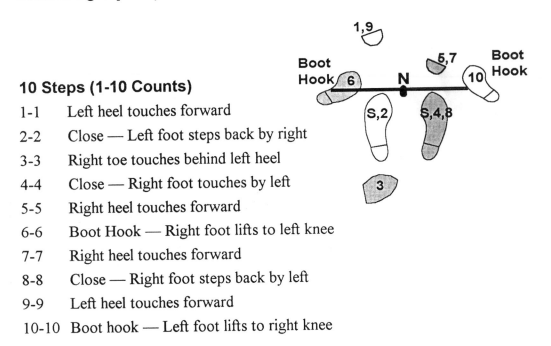

10 Steps (1-10 Counts)

1-1   Left heel touches forward

2-2   Close — Left foot steps back by right

3-3   Right toe touches behind left heel

4-4   Close — Right foot touches by left

5-5   Right heel touches forward

6-6   Boot Hook — Right foot lifts to left knee

7-7   Right heel touches forward

8-8   Close — Right foot steps back by left

9-9   Left heel touches forward

10-10 Boot hook — Left foot lifts to right knee

Left Triple Step, Right Triple Step, Left Triple Step, Right Triple Step (11-18 Counts)

11-1   Left foot steps forward

11-&   Right toe touches forward

12-2   Left foot steps forward

13-3   Right foot steps forward

13-&   Left toe touches forward

14-4   Right foot steps forward

15-1   Left foot steps forward

15-&   Right toe touches forward

16-2   Left foot steps forward

17-3   Right foot steps forward

17-&   Left toe touches forward

18-4   Right foot steps forward

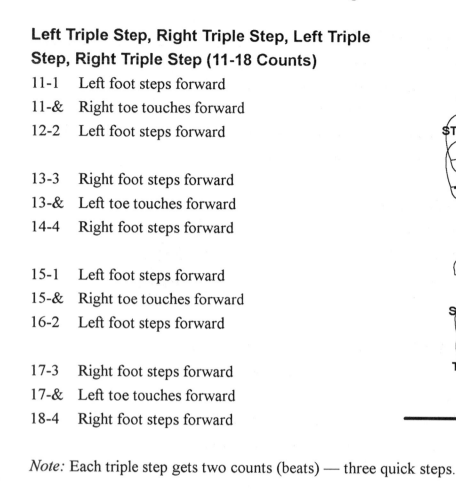

Note: Each triple step gets two counts (beats) — three quick steps.

To embellish the 10-Step, any of the Two-Step turns can be performed during the four shuffle steps. The key to 10-Step turns is to have the lady finish the turn square to the line of dance, either facing the line of dance on the right side, left side, in front of, or behind the gentleman.

Trick:

The 10-Step is a dance that prompts many bands to discover how fast the dancers can move. So, the band increases the tempo (speed) of the music near the end of the dance. To do the 10-Step faster, take small steps and abbreviate the moves. For example, instead of the boot hook going to the knee, just hook to ankle height.

APPLE JACK — STARTER

Line dance, very easy, 4 walls — 26 counts

Music: "Mercury Blues" by Alan Jackson, "Fireman" by George Strait

Description: Fun easy dance for beginners. The original APPLE JACK has some difficult double fans that even the expert dancers have to work hard to learn. This is a good example of a fun dance being modified.

Fan Left, Fan Right (1-4 Counts)

1-1   Left toe swivels left

2-2   Left toe swivels to front

3-3   Right toe swivels right

4-4   Right toe swivels to front

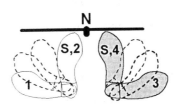

Fan Left 2Xs (5-8 Counts)

5-1   Left toe swivels left

6-2   Left toe swivels to front

7-3   Left toe swivels left

8-4   Left toe swivels to front

Fan Right 2Xs (9-12 Counts)

9-1   Right toe swivels right

10-2   Right toe swivels to front

11-3   Right toe swivels right

12-4   Right toe swivels to front

Fan Left, Fan Right (13-16 Counts)

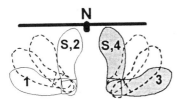

13-1   Left toe swivels left

14-2   Left toe swivels to front

15-3   Right toe swivels right

16-4   Right toe swivels to front

Heel, Toe, Step, Toe (17-20 Counts)

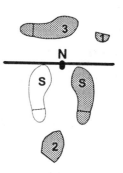

17-1   Right heel touches forward

18-2   Right toe touches back by left heel

19-3   Right foot steps forward, turning 1/4 right

20-4   Left toe touches left

Step, Touch, Step, Step (21-24 Counts)

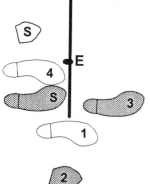

21-1   Left foot steps across (in front) right foot

22-2   Right toe touches right side

23-3   Right foot steps across (in front) left foot

24-4   Left foot steps back

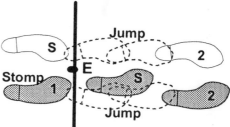

Close, Jump (25-26 Counts)

25-1   Close — Right foot stomps by left

26-2   Jump forward landing with feet together — Clap

BLACK VELVET (SKEE BUMPUS)

Line dance, easy, 2 walls — 40 counts

Music: "Black Velvet" by Robin Lee, "Slow Hand" by Conway Twitty

Description: Slow dance with lots of opportunity for self expression, especially with the points at the beginning of the dance.

Point Close (1-8 Counts)

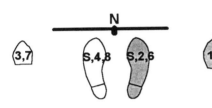

1-1 Point right — Right toe touches to the right side

2-2 Close — Right foot back to center

3-3 Point left — Left toe touches to left side

4-4 Close — Left foot back to center

5-5 Point right — Right toe touches to right side

6-6 Close — Right foot back to center

7-7 Point left — Left toe touches to left side

8-8 Close — Left foot back to center

Kick Ball Change 2Xs (9-12 Counts)

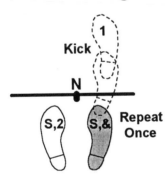

9-1 Right foot kicks forward

10-& Close — Right foot steps by left

10-2 Left foot steps in place

11-3 Right foot kicks forward

12-& Close — Right foot steps by left

12-4 Left foot steps in place

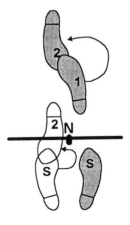

Turn (13-14 Counts)

13-1 Right foot steps forward

14-2 Turn 1/2 to the left

Kick Ball Change 2Xs (15-18 Counts)

15-1   Right foot kicks forward

16-&   Close — Right foot steps back by left

16-2   Left foot steps in place

17-3   Right foot kicks forward

18-&   Close — Right foot steps back by left

18-4   Left foot steps in place

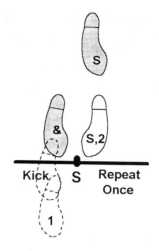

Turn (19-20 Counts)

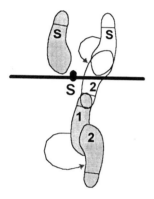

19-1   Right foot steps forward

20-2   Turn 1/2 to left

Triple Steps (21-24 Counts)

21-1   Right foot steps forward

21-&   Left foot steps forward

22-2   Right foot steps forward

23-3   Left foot steps forward

23-&   Right foot steps forward

24-4   Left foot steps forward

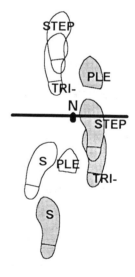

Turn (25-26 Counts)

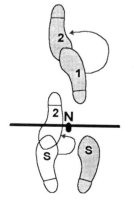

25-1   Right foot steps forward

26-2   Turn 1/2 to left

Triple Steps (27-30 Counts)

27-1   Right foot steps forward

27-&   Left foot steps forward

28-2   Right foot steps forward

29-3   Left foot steps forward

29-&   Right foot steps forward

30-4   Left foot steps forward

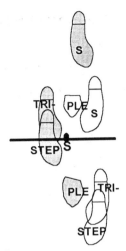

Turn (31-32 Counts)

31-1   Right foot steps forward

32-2   Turn 1/2 left

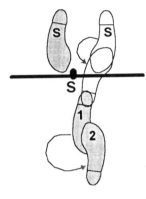

Jazz Boxes (33-40 Counts)

33-1   Right foot crosses over left

34-2   Left foot steps back

35-3   Right foot steps right

36-4   Stomp left foot

37-5   Right foot crosses over left

38-6   Left foot steps back

39-7   Right foot steps right

40-8   Stomp left foot

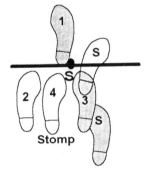

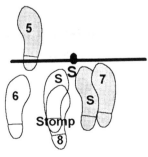

COPPERHEAD ROAD — EUROPEAN STYLE

Line dance, very easy, 4 walls — 28 counts

Music: "Copperhead Road" by Steve Earle, "Bubba Shot The Jukebox" by Mark Chesnutt, "Wrong Side Of Memphis" by Trisha Yearwood

Description: Not really sure where the name for this variation of the COPPER-HEAD ROAD originated. Mark Collard, DJ for an Antelope Valley radio station, says it is the European style of COPPERHEAD ROAD. The jump-stomp with the left foot kicking back makes this an easy fun, dance. Also, the variations that can be added are too numerous to count.

Heel, Close, Heel, Close (1-4 Counts)

1-1	Right heel touches forward
2-2	Close — Right foot steps back to center
3-3	Left heel touches forward
4-4	Close — Left foot steps back to center

Heel, Close, Heel, Close (5-8 Counts)

5-1 Right heel touches forward

6-2 Close — Right foot steps back to center

7-3 Left heel touches forward

8-4 Close — Left foot steps back to close

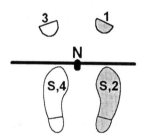

Jump-Stomp-Kick, Step, Step, Step (9-12 Counts)

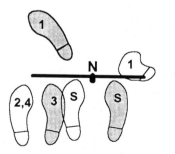

9-1	Jump with right foot crossing in front of left foot while left foot kicks back (the right foot lands with a stomp)
10-2	Left foot steps back
11-3	Right foot steps by left
12-4	Right foot steps by right
Note:	With these Jump-Stomp-Kick steps you can stomp on counts 3 and 4. Or, you can just pause.

Jump-Stomp-Kick, Step, Step, Step (13-16 Counts)

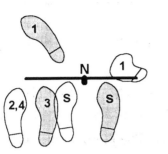

13-1   Jump with right foot crossing in front of left while left foot kicks back of right leg (the right   foot lands with a stomp)

14-2   Left foot steps back

15-3   Right foot steps by left

16-4   Left foot steps by right

Heel, Close, Heel, Close (17-20 Counts)

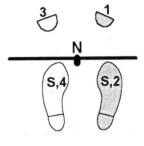

17-1   Right heel touches forward

18-2   Close — Right foot steps back by left

19-3   Left heel touches forward

20-4   Close — Left foot steps back by right

Heel, Close, Heel, Close (21-24 Counts)

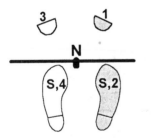

21-1   Right heel touches forward

22-2   Close — Right foot steps back by left

23-3   Left heel touches forward

24-4   Close — left foot steps back by right

Jump-Stomp-Kick-Turn, Step, Step, Step (25-28 Counts)

25-1   Jump with right foot crossing in front of left foot turning 1/4 left while left foot kicks back of right leg (the right foot lands with a stomp)

26-2   Left foot steps back

27-3   Right foot steps by left

28-4   Left foot steps by right

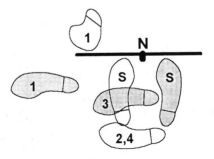

COWBOY BOOGIE or WATERGATE

Line dance, very easy, 4 walls — 24 counts

Music: "Swingin'" by John Anderson, "Redneck Girl" by The Bellamy Brothers, "All My Rowdy Friends" by Hank Williams Jr.

Description: This is a very simple dance and one of the first dances you'll want to learn. The vines with brushes and hip rocks allow for some interesting variations.

Grapevine Right, Brush (1-4 Counts)

1-1   Right foot steps right

2-2   Left foot steps behind right foot

3-3   Right foot steps right

4-4   Left foot brushes by right foot and clap

Grapevine Left, Brush (5-8 Count)

5-1   Left foot steps left

6-2   Right foot steps behind left foot

7-3   Left foot steps left

8-4   Right foot brushes by left foot and clap

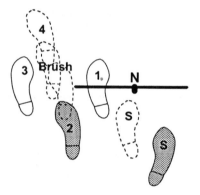

Step, Brush, Step, Brush (9-12 Count)

9-1   Right foot steps forward

10-2   Left foot brushes by right foot and clap

11-3   Left foot steps forward

12-4   Right foot brushes by left foot and clap

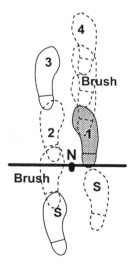

Back, Forward (13-16 Counts)

13-1   Right foot steps back

14-2   Left foot steps back

15-3   Right foot steps back

16-4   Left foot steps forward

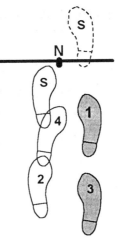

Rock, Hips, Rock, Hips (17-20 Counts)

17-1   Left foot rocks forward and bump hips left

18-2   Bump hips left

19-3   Right foot rocks back

20-4   Bump hips right and bump hips left

Swing Hips, Turn (21-24 Counts)

21-1   Left hip bumps forward

22-2   Right hip bumps back

23-3   Left hip bumps forward

24-4   Right foot brushes floor by left foot, turning 1/4 left

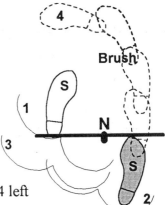

With any easy line dance, the opportunities for embellishments increase. Some of the variations performed after the step touches include: going back with stomps, Freeze, Pee Wee, attitude, shoot out, space out, and the horse ride. Usually, someone in the group will call out the next variation.

ELECTRIC SLIDE

Line dance, very easy, 4 walls—18 counts

Music: "Pink Cadillac" by Southern Pacific, "Stroking" by Clarence Carter, "Electric Slide" by M.C. Hammer

Description: The ELECTRIC SLIDE is one of the first dances folks want to learn. It is one of the easiest line dances to learn and perform. The dance traces an upside down "L" shape on the floor.

Step, Slide, Step, Slide, Step, Touch (1-4 Counts)

1-1   Right foot steps to the right side

1-&   Left foot slides to right foot

2-2   Right foot steps right

2-&   Left foot slides to right foot

3-3   Right foot steps right

4-4   Lift left foot and touch by right foot

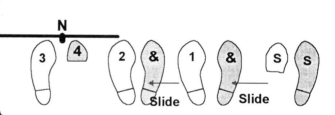

Step, Slide, Step, Slide, Step, Touch (5-8 counts)

5-1   Left foot steps to the left

5-&   Right foot slides to left

6-2   Left foot steps left

6-&   Right foot slides to left

7-3   Left foot steps left

8-4   Right foot touches by left

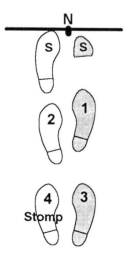

Walk Back (9-12 Counts)

9-1   Right foot steps back

10-2   Left foot steps back

11-3   Right foot steps back

12-4   Stomp left foot — Clap is optional

Step, Touch, Step, Step (13-16 Counts)

13-1 Left foot steps forward

14-2 Right foot touches behind left, dropping left knee

15-3 Right foot steps to right side

16-4 Left foot touches back

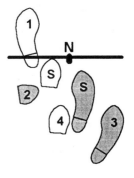

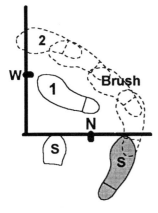

Turn, Brush (17-18 Counts)

17-1 Left foot steps forward, turning 1/4 right

18-2 Right foot brushes by left foot

Notes: The ELECTRIC SLIDE is very a popular and simple line dance. As a result, many embellishments are added to the dance. For example, full turns can replace the movements to the left and/or right. You even can do a turn on the three back steps. You also can do a grapevine right and/or left for the side movements.

Or, instead of doing the left and right moves, step out left with a long step and slowly drag the right foot to left. Then, the same move can be used going back the other direction. The point is to have fun.

Or, in the fourth set of moves, rock forward twice and rock back twice.

FREEZE

Line dance, easy, 4 walls — 16 counts

Music: "Stand Up" by Mel McDaniel, "Whiskey Ain't Workin'" by Travis Tritt, "Harper Valley PTA" by Jeannie C. Riley

Description: Good line dance for beginners — Lots of hops.

Vine Right, Hop (1-4 Counts)

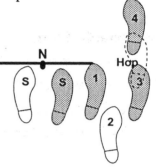

1-1   Right foot steps right

2-2   Left foot steps behind right foot

3-3   Right foot steps right

4-4   Hop on right foot, kicking left foot forward

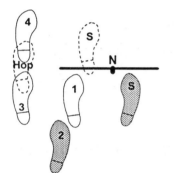

Vine Left, Hop (5-8 Counts)

5-1   Left foot steps left

6-2   Right foot steps behind left

7-3   Left foot steps left

8-4   Hop on left foot, kicking right foot forward

Step, Step, Step, Hop (9-12 Counts)

9-1   Right foot steps back

10-2   Left foot steps back

11-3   Right foot steps back

12-4   Right foot hops forward, kicking left foot forward

Step, Rock, Rock, Hop (13-16 Counts)

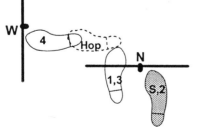

13-1   Left foot steps forward

14-2   Rock back on right foot

15-3   Rock forward on left foot

16-4   Left foot hops, turning 1/4 left

SLIDIN' HOME

Line dance, very easy, 4 walls — 44 counts

Music: "Take It Easy" by Reba McEntire, "If It Wasn't For Her I Wouldn't Have You" by Daron Norwood

Description: Watching the young kids perform this dance is enjoyable.

Step, Touch, Step, Touch, Step, Together, Step, Touch (1-8 Counts)

1-1	Right foot steps right
2-2	Left toe touches by right
3-3	Left foot steps left
4-4	Right toe touches by left

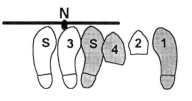

5-1	Right foot steps right
6-2	Left foot steps to right foot
7-3	Right foot steps right
8-4	Left toe touches by right

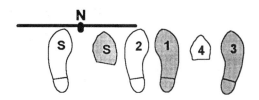

Step, Touch, Step, Touch, Step, Together, Step, Touch (9-16 Counts)

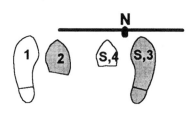

9-1	Left foot steps left
10-2	Right toe touches by left
11-3	Right foot steps right
12-4	Left toe touches by right

13-1	Left foot steps left
14-2	Right foot steps to left
15-3	Left foot steps left
16-4	Right toe touches by left

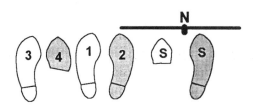

Step, Touch, Step, Touch, Step, Together, Step, Touch (17-24 Counts)

17-1 Right foot steps forward

18-2 Left toe touches by right

19-3 Left foot steps back

20-4 Right toe touches by left

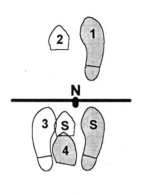

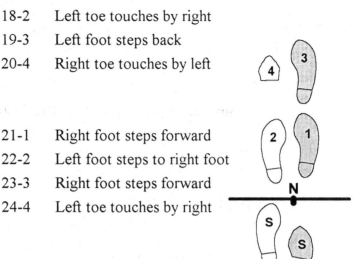

21-1 Right foot steps forward

22-2 Left foot steps to right foot

23-3 Right foot steps forward

24-4 Left toe touches by right

Step, Touch, Step, Touch, Step, Together, Step, Touch (25-32 Counts)

25-1 Left foot steps back

26-2 Right toe touches by left

27-3 Right foot steps forward

28-4 Left toe touches by right

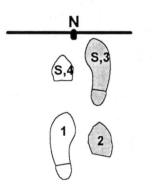

29-1 Left foot steps back

30-2 Right foot steps to left foot

31-3 Left foot steps back

32-4 Right foot steps by left

Step, Shimmy, Hold (33-36 Counts)

33-1 Right foot steps right — Extended step

34-2 Left foot slides right — Shimmy shoulders

35-3 Left foot slides right — Shimmy shoulders

36-4 Hold and clap

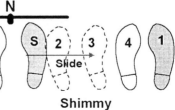

Shimmy

Step, Shimmy, Hold (37-40 Counts)

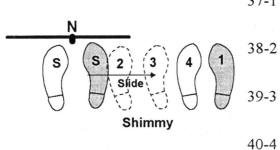

37-1	Right foot steps right — Extended step
38-2	Left foot slides right — Shimmy shoulders
39-3	Left foot slides right — Shimmy shoulders
40-4	Hold and Clap

Step, Slide, Step, Slide (41-44 Counts)

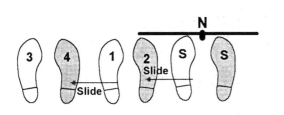

41-1	Left foot steps left
42-2	Right foot slides left
43-3	Left foot steps left
44-4	Right foot slides left

Step, Slide, Turn, Stomp (45-48 Counts)

45-1   Left foot steps left

46-2   Right foot slides left

47-3   Left foot steps, turning 1/4 left

48-4   Right foot stomps by left

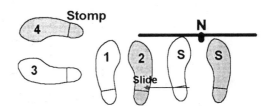

TENNESSEE TWISTER

Line dance, easy, 2 walls — 32 counts

Music: "Wildman" by Ricky Van Shelton, "Take It Back" by Reba McEntire, "What Part Of No" by Lorrie Morgan

Description: For some reason or another, it is our understanding that the TENNESSEE TWISTER originated in Ohio. So, why is it named TENNESSEE TWISTER?

Swivel 4Xs (1-4 Counts)

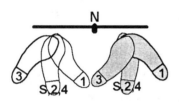

1-1	Swivel both heels to the right
2-2	Swivel both heels back to center
3-3	Swivel both heels to the left
4-4	Swivel both heels back to center

Swivel, Twist, Twist, Swivel (5-8 Counts)

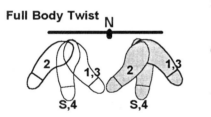

5-1	Swivel right — Swivel heels to the right as your knees go to the left
6-2	Twist left — Twist heels to the left as your knees go to the right
7-3	Twist right — Twist heels to the right as your knees go to the left

8-4   Swivel, left — Swivel heels to center as your knees go to the right

Note: Bend your knees to exaggerate the twisting motion.

Heel, Heel, Toe, Toe (9-12 Counts)

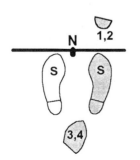

9-1	Right heel touches forward
10-2	Right heel touches forward
11-3	Right toe touches back
12-4	Right toe touches back

Step, Shimmy, Hold (37-40 Counts)

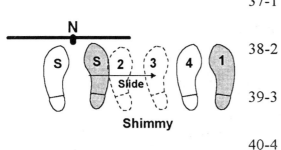

Shimmy

37-1	Right foot steps right — Extended step
38-2	Left foot slides right — Shimmy shoulders
39-3	Left foot slides right — Shimmy shoulders
40-4	Hold and Clap

Step, Slide, Step, Slide (41-44 Counts)

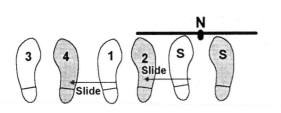

41-1	Left foot steps left
42-2	Right foot slides left
43-3	Left foot steps left
44-4	Right foot slides left

Step, Slide, Turn, Stomp (45-48 Counts)

45-1　Left foot steps left

46-2　Right foot slides left

47-3　Left foot steps, turning 1/4 left

48-4　Right foot stomps by left

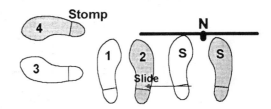

TENNESSEE TWISTER

Line dance, easy, 2 walls — 32 counts

Music: "Wildman" by Ricky Van Shelton, "Take It Back" by Reba McEntire, "What Part Of No" by Lorrie Morgan

Description: For some reason or another, it is our understanding that the TENNESSEE TWISTER originated in Ohio. So, why is it named TENNESSEE TWISTER?

Swivel 4Xs (1-4 Counts)

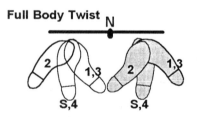

1-1	Swivel both heels to the right
2-2	Swivel both heels back to center
3-3	Swivel both heels to the left
4-4	Swivel both heels back to center

Swivel, Twist, Twist, Swivel (5-8 Counts)

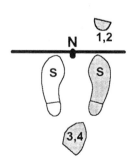

Full Body Twist

5-1	Swivel right — Swivel heels to the right as your knees go to the left
6-2	Twist left — Twist heels to the left as your knees go to the right
7-3	Twist right — Twist heels to the right as your knees go to the left

8-4   Swivel, left — Swivel heels to center as your knees go to the right

Note: Bend your knees to exaggerate the twisting motion.

Heel, Heel, Toe, Toe (9-12 Counts)

9-1	Right heel touches forward
10-2	Right heel touches forward
11-3	Right toe touches back
12-4	Right toe touches back

Step, Drag, Step, Drag (13-16 Counts)

13-1 Right foot steps forward

14-2 Left foot drags to right — Keeping left foot crossed behind right

15-3 Right foot steps forward

16-4 Left foot drags to right — Keeping left foot crossed behind right

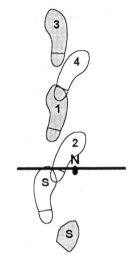

Step, Turn, Step, Step (17-20 Counts)

17-1 Right foot steps forward

18-2 Turn 1/2 to the right on right foot, swinging left foot around

19-3 Left foot steps by right

20-4 Right foot steps behind left

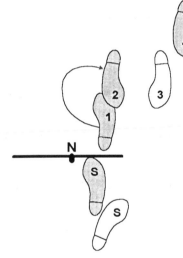

Step, Drag, Step, Turn (21-24 Counts)

21-1 Left foot steps forward

22-2 Right foot drags to left — Keeping right foot crossed behind left

23-3 Left foot steps forward

24-4 Turn 1/2 to the left on the left foot, swinging right foot around

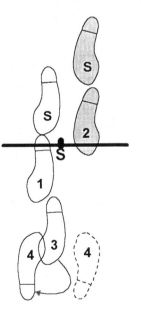

Vine Right, Turn (25- 28 Counts)

25-1　　Right foot steps right

26-2　　Left foot steps behind right

27-1　　Right foot steps right

28-4　　Right foot scoots, turning 1/2 right

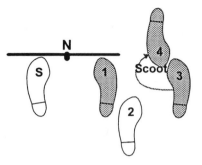

Vine Left (29-32 Counts)

29-1　　Left foot steps left

30-2　　Right foot steps behind left

31-3　　Left foot steps left

32-4　　Right foot stomps by left

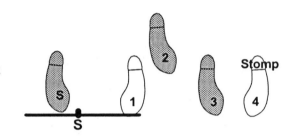

Chapter 4
Easy Line Dances

BERRY JAM

Line dance, easy, 4 walls — 32 counts

Music: "Hard Way to Make a Living" by The Bellamy Brothers, "Queen of Memphis" by Confederate Railroad, "Honky Tonk Attitude" by Joe Diffie

Description: BERRY JAM is a line dance with an interesting story. Knott's Berry Farm® of Buena Park, Calif., promoted a TUSH PUSH contest in the spring of 1993. All the dance clubs and dancing establishments in Southern California were asked to hold preliminary contests.

On the big day of the finals, all the contestants were judged on their ability to dance the TUSH PUSH. Then, BERRY JAM was introduced and taught to the finalists. The dancers were challenged to embellish and add their style to a dance they had never before danced. What a challenge!

Thus, the world now has BERRY JAM — a fun, little, easy dance. Enjoy it!

Boot Hook Right (1-4 Counts)

1-1   Right heel touches forward

2-2   Right foot lifts to left knee

3-3   Right heel touches forward

4-4   Right toe touches by left heel

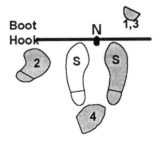

Grapevine Right (5-8 Counts)

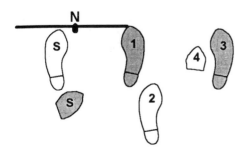

5-1   Right foot sides to the right side

6-2   Left foot steps behind right foot

7-3   Right foot steps right

8-4   Left toe touches by right heel

Boot Hook Left (9-12 Counts)

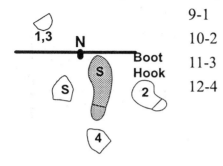

9-1   Left heel touches forward

10-2   Left foot lifts to right knee

11-3   Left heel touches forward

12-4   Left toe touches by right heel

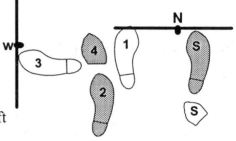

Grapevine Left (13-16 Counts)

13-1   Left foot steps left

14-2   Right foot steps behind left foot

15-3   Left foot steps left, turning 1/4 to the left

16-4   Right toe touches floor by left heel

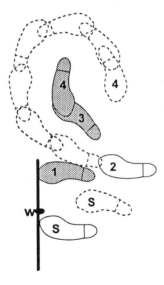

Grapevine Right (17-20 Counts)

17-1   Right foot steps right

18-2   Left foot steps behind right

19-3   Right foot steps right turning right slightly

20-4   Left foot swings around, turning 3/4 right

Step, Rock, Charleston (21-24 Counts)

21-1   Left foot steps forward

22-2   Right foot rocks back

23-3   Left foot steps forward

24-4   Right foot kicks forward, clap hands

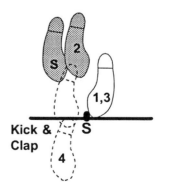

Step, Touch, Step, Brush (25-28 Counts)

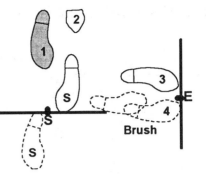

25-1 Right foot steps back

26-2 Left toe touches back

27-3 Left foot steps forward, turning 1/4 left

28-4 Right foot brushes left

Toe, Heel, Toe, Heel (29-32 Counts)

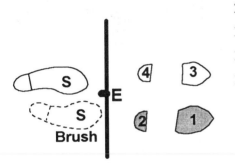

29-1 Tap — Right toe touches forward

30-2 Right heel steps down

31-3 Tap — Left toe touches forward

32-4 Left heel steps down

CHATTAHOOCHIE

Line dance, easy , 4 walls — 28 counts

Music: "Chattahoochie River" by Alan Jackson

Left Boot Hook (1-4 Counts)

1-1   Left heel touches forward

2-2   Left heel lifts to right knee

3-3   Left heel touches forward

4-4   Close — Left foot steps by right

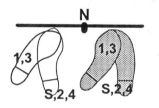

Swivel Left 2Xs (5-8 Counts)

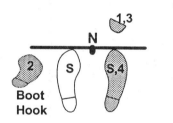

5-1   Swivel both heels to left

6-2   Swivel both heels to center

7-3   Swivel both heels to left

8-4   Swivel both heels to center

Right Boot Hook (9-12 Counts)

9-1   Right heel touches forward

10-2   Right heel lifts to left knee

11-3   Right heel touches forward

12-4   Close — Right foot steps by left

Swivel Right 2Xs (13-16 Counts)

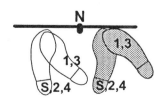

13-1   Swivel both heels to right

14-2   Swivel both heels to center

15-3   Swivel both heels to right

16-4   Swivel both heels to center

Slap Boots (17-20 Counts)

17-1   Right foot steps right

18-2   Left foot lifts behind right knee
and slap boot with right hand

19-3   Left foot steps left

20-4   Right foot lifts behind left knee
and slap boot with left hand

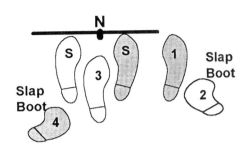

Grapevine Right , Turn, Stomp (21-24 Counts)

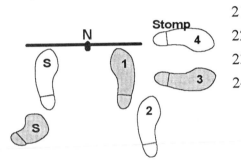

21-1   Right foot steps right

22-2   Left foot steps behind right

23-3   Right foot steps right, turning 1/4 right

24-4   Left foot stomps by right

Step Back, Stomp (25-28 Counts)

25-1   Left steps back

26-2   Right foot steps back

27-3   Left foot steps back

28-4   Right foot stomps by left

COWGIRL DANCE

Line dance, moderately easy, 4 walls — 56 counts

Music: "Cowgirl Dance" by Ron Marshall, "Take It Back" (slow) by Reba McEntire

Choreographer: Patsy Phillips of Lancaster, California

Description: The COWGIRL DANCE was choreographed for Ron Marshall's song, "Cowgirl Dance". It is really a great-looking dance with that song, but can be done with "Take It Back". The dance has many innovative moves that make it fun.

Strut Steps (1-8 Counts)

1-1 Right heel, small step forward with toe up

2-2 Right toes slaps down

3-3 Left heel, small step forward with toe up

4-4 Left toe slaps down

5-5 Right heel, small step forward with toe up

6-6 Right toe slaps down

7-7 Left heel, small step forward with toe up

8-8 Left toe slaps down

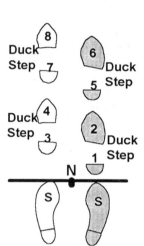

Point Right Side (9-12 Counts)

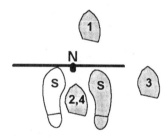

9-1 Right toe touches forward

10-2 Close — Right toe touches by left foot

11-3 Right toe touches right side — Toe facing forward

12-4 Close — Right toe touches by left foot

Step, Slide, Hold (13-16 Counts)

13-1 Right foot steps right

14-2&3 Left foot slides to right — Lift arms out to side and shimmy shoulders — 2 counts

16-4 Hold — Clap

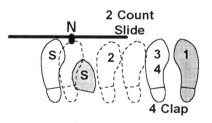

Point Left Side (17-20 Counts)

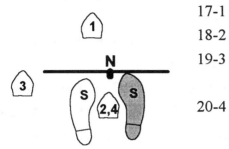

17-1 Left toe touches forward

18-2 Close — Left toe touches by right foot

19-3 Left toe touches left side — Toes facing forward

20-4 Close — Left toe touches by right foot

Step, Slide, Hold (21-24 Counts)

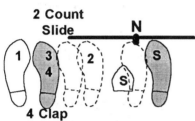

21-1 Left foot steps left

22-2&3 Right foot slides to left, lift arms out to side and shimmy shoulders — 2 counts

24-4 Hold — Clap

Step, Turn, Step, Turn, Step, Turn (25-32 Counts)

25-1 Right foot steps forward

26-2 Turn 1/2 to left

27-3 Right foot steps forward

28-4 Turn 1/2 to left

29-5 Right foot steps forward

30-6 Turn 1/4 to left

31-7 Right foot slides to left while doing last turn

32-8 Hold — Clap

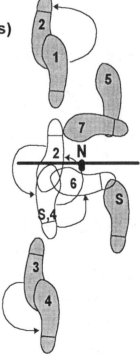

Boot Hook, Step, Slide, Step, Slide, Step, Touches (33-40 Counts)

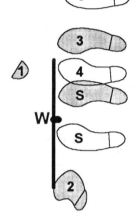

33-1	Right heel touches forward
34-2	Right boot hook — Right heel touches left knee
35-3	Right foot steps right
36-4	Left foot slides right
37-5	Right foot steps right
38-6	Left foot slides right
39-7	Right foot steps right
40-8	Left toe touches by right

Boot Hook, Step, Slide, Step, Slide, Step, Touches (41-48 Counts)

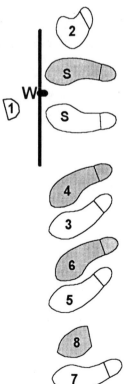

41-1	Left heel touches forward
42-2	Left boot hook — Left heel touches by right knee
43-3	Left foot steps left
44-4	Right foot slides left
45-5	Left foot steps left
46-6	Right foot slides left
47-7	Left foot steps left
48-8	Right toe touches by left

Heel, Close, Heel, Close (49-52 Counts)

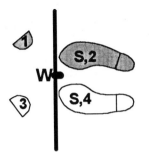

49-1 Right heel touches forward

50-2 Close — Right foot back to center

51-3 Left heel touches forward

52-4 Close — Left foot back to center

Prance (53-56 Counts)

53-1&2 Stand with feet close, bend both knees, swing knees left and right while swinging body down — Shift weight right, then left, making hips move.

55-3&4 Stand with feet close, bend both knees, swing knees left and right while swinging body up — Shifting weight left, then right, making hips move.

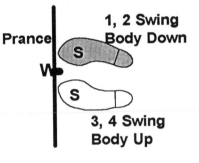

Note: For the men's prance, some teachers suggest repeating right heel, left heel. The choreographer's intent was for the men to prance with the ladies.

FLYING 8

Line dance, moderately easy, 2 walls — 20 counts

Music: "Freeze Frame" by J. Giles Band, "Heartland" by George Strait, "Drivin' My Life Away" by Eddie Rabbit, "Cherokee Fiddle" (slow) by Johnny Lee

Description: This is a very aerobic line dance. The FLYING 8 covers lots of floor going north and south. The scoot is sometimes referred to as a hop, but it is really a scoot or slide. For each scoot, clap at the same time. While scooting on one foot, the opposite foot hitches or kicks forward.

FLYING 8 has an interesting and different beginning. When you first learn the dance, take a couple of walking steps forward. You actually start the dance by scooting. This is one dance that you join and follow the dance leader. FLYING 8 is shown here starting on the right foot, but it is just as easy to begin on the left.

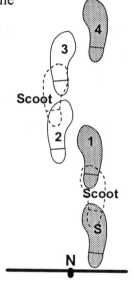

Scoot, Step, Scoot, Step (1-4 Counts)

1-1   Right foot scoots forward — Clap

2-2   Left foot steps forward

3-3   Left foot scoots forward — Clap

4-4   Right foot steps forward

Scoot, Vine Left (5-8 Counts)

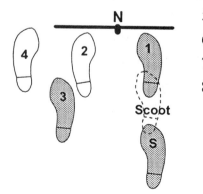

5-1   Right foot scoots forward — Clap

6-2   Left foot steps left

7-3   Right foot steps behind left foot

8-4   Left foot steps left

Scoot, Grapevine Right (9-12 Counts)

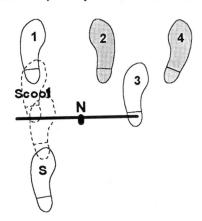

9-1	Left foot scoots forward — Clap
10-2	Right foot steps right
11-3	Left foot steps behind right
12-4	Right foot steps right

Scoot, Vine Left (13-16 Counts)

13-1	Right foot scoots, turning 1/4
14-2	Left foot steps left
15-3	Right foot steps behind left
16-4	Left foot steps left

right

Turn, Step, Rock, Step (17-20 Counts)

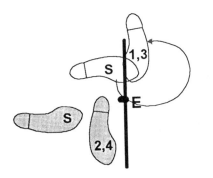

17-1   Turn 3/4 left — On the left foot

Note: You will be facing the opposite direction to start the next wall.

18-2   Right foot steps forward

19-3   Left foot rocks back

20-4   Right foot steps forward

Note: Clapping really helps with your timing.

NEON MOON

Line dance, easy Cha-Cha, 2 walls — 34 counts

Music: Any slow Cha-Cha music, "Neon Moon" by Brooks and Dunn

Description: A reverse Cha-Cha step is used in the NEON MOON. The Cha-Cha steps are performed before the two slower steps. Recall that a Cha-Cha step is a step-step-triple step. A triple step is a left-right-left or right-left-right performed in 2 counts.

Point, Close, Point, Close (1-4 Counts)

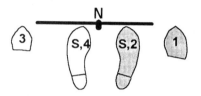

1-1 Right toe touches right

2-2 Close — Right foot steps back to center

3-3 Left toe touches left

4-4 Close — Left foot steps back to center

Sweeping Left Turn (5-8 Counts)

5-1 Swing right foot out in front and around

6-2 Turn 1/2 to the left

7-3 Close — Right foot steps by left

8-4 Both heels down

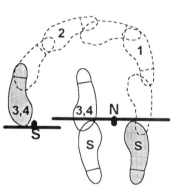

Point, Close, Point, Close (9-12 Counts)

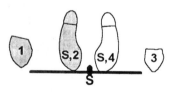

9-1   Right toe touches right

10-2   Close — Right foot steps back to the center

11-3   Left toe touches left

12-4   Close — Left foot steps back to the center

Sweeping Left Turn (13-16 Counts)

13-1   Swing right foot out in front and around

14-2   Turn 1/2 to the left

15-3   Close — Right foot steps by left

16-4   Both heels down

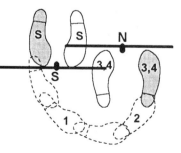

Triple Step, Rock, Step (17-20 Counts)

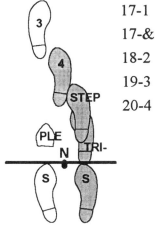

17-1	Right foot steps forward
17-&	Left foot steps forward
18-2	Right foot steps forward
19-3	Left foot rocks forward
20-4	Right foot steps back

Triple Step, Rock, Forward (21-24 Counts)

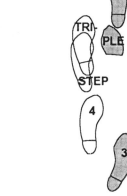

21-1	Left foot steps back
21-&	Right foot steps back
22-2	Left foot steps back
23-3	Right foot rocks back
24-4	Left foot steps forward

Rock, Recovery, Back, Recovery (25-28 Counts)

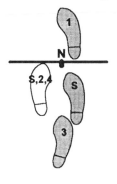

25-1	Right foot rocks forward
26-2	Recovery — Shift weight to the left foot
27-3	Right foot steps back
28-4	Recovery — Shift weight to the left foot

Turning Triple Step, Rock, Step (29-32 Counts)

29-1	Right foot steps forward, turning 1/4 left
29-&	Left foot steps forward
30-2	Right foot steps back, turning 1/4 left
31-3	Left foot rocks back
32-4	Right foot steps forward

Left Triple Step (33-34 Counts)

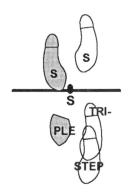

33-1	Left foot steps forward
33-&	Right foot steps forward
34-2	Left foot steps forward

TEXAS COUNTY LINE

Line dance, easy Cha-Cha, 4 walls — 20 counts

Music: Any Cha-Cha music, "Neon Moon" by Brooks and Dunn, "If I Said You Have A Beautiful Body Would You Hold It Against Me" by The Bellamy Brothers, "Cross My Broken Heart" by Suzy Bogguss

Description: This is a very simple and easy Cha-Cha line dance. It's an excellent dance to teach the basic Cha-Cha step and Cha-Cha turns. The turns do take some concentration.

Note: Remember the Cha-Cha step in this dance is the same as a triple step. The illustrations are shown as "Cha-Cha" instead of the usual "TRI- PLE STEP" for variety and because the dance really has a Cha-Cha feel to it.

Cha-Cha Step (1-4 Counts)

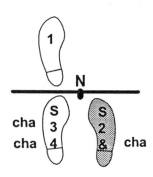

1-1	Left foot rocks forward
2-2	Right foot rocks back
3-3	Step left
3-&	Step right
4-4	Step left

Turning One-Half Left Cha-Cha Step (5-8 Counts)

5-1	Right foot rocks back
6-2	Left foot rocks back
7-3	Step right, turning 1/4 left
7-&	Step left, turning 1/4 left
8-4	Step right

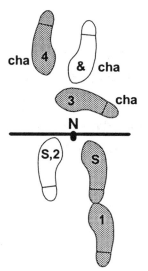

Turning One-Half Right Cha-Cha Step (9-12 Counts)

9-1   Left foot rocks back

10-2   Right foot rocks forward

11-3   Step left, turning 1/4 right

11-&   Step right, turning 1/4 right

12-4   Step left

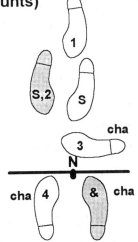

Turning One-Quarter Left Cha-Cha Step (13-16 Counts)

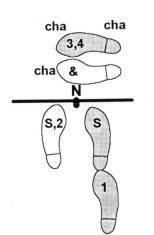

13-1   Right foot rocks back

14-2   Left foot rocks forward

15-3   Step right, turning 1/4 to the left

15-&   Step left

16-4   Step right

Step, Turn, Step, Turn (17-20 Counts)

17-1   Left toe touches forward — Turning 1/2 right

18-2   Right foot steps back by left

19-3   Left foot steps forward — Turning 1/2 right

20-4   Right foot steps back by left

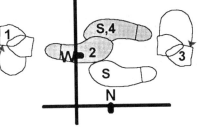

WALTZ ACROSS TEXAS

Line dance, easy waltz, 1 wall — 48 counts

Music: any waltz, "Waltz Across Texas" by Willie Nelson, "Something in Red" by Lorrie Morgan, "Tennessee Waltz" by Lacy J. Dalton, "You Look So Good in Love" by George Strait, "Here's a Quarter" by Travis Tritt, "High Lonesome" by Randy Travis

Description: This easy waltz line dance teaches turns. The waltz is a graceful, slow, flowing dance that should be expressed with charm, elegance, and poise.

Note: In a waltz, many of the steps are performed in place; only the weight is shifted. The bolder moves are on the first and fourth counts.

Two Twinkles (1-6 Counts)

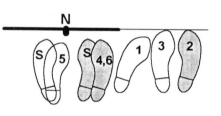

1-1	Left foot crosses over right
2-2	Right foot steps right
3-3	Close — Left foot steps by right
4-4	Right foot crosses over left
5-5	Left foot steps left
6-6	Close — Right foot steps by left

Waltz Forward (7-12 Counts)

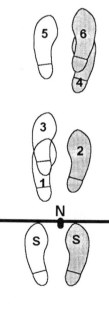

7-1	Left foot steps forward
8-2	Right foot steps to the left foot
9-3	Left foot steps forward, slightly
10-4	Right foot steps forward
11-5	Left foot steps forward to right foot
12-6	Right foot steps forward, slightly

Waltz Back (13-18 Counts)

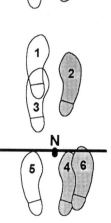

13-1	Left foot steps backward
14-2	Right foot steps to left foot
15-3	Left foot steps back, slightly
16-4	Right foot steps back
17-5	Left foot steps back to right foot
18-6	Right foot steps back, slightly

Waltz to the Left and Pivoting Left — 9 Counts (19-27 Counts)

19-1   Left foot steps left, pivoting 1/4 left

20-2   Right foot steps over left, pivoting 1/2 left

21-3   Left foot steps behind, pivoting 1/4 left

22-4   Right foot crosses over left

23-5   Left foot steps back and to the left

24-6   Right foot steps behind left

25-7   Left foot steps back

26-8   Right foot steps to left foot

27-9   Left foot rocks back

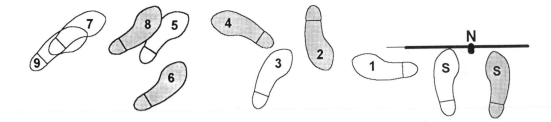

Waltz to the Right and Pivoting Right — 9 Counts (28-36 Counts)

28-1   Right foot steps right, pivoting 1/4 right

29-2   Left foot steps over right, pivoting 1/2 right

30-3   Right foot steps behind left, pivoting 1/4 right

31-4   Left foot crosses over right

32-5   Right foot steps back

33-6   Left foot steps behind right

34-7   Right foot steps right

35-8   Left foot steps to right foot

36-9   Right foot steps in place

Waltz Diagonally and Pivot (37-42 Counts)

37-1   Left foot steps out diagonally to left

38-2   Right foot crosses over left, pivoting 1/4 left

39-3   Left foot steps back of right, pivoting 1/4 left

40-4   Right foot steps back

41-5   Left foot steps back

42-6   Right foot steps back

Waltz Diagonally and Pivot (43-48 Counts)

43-1   Left foot steps out diagonally to the left

44-2   Right foot crosses over left, pivoting 1/4 left

45-3   Left foot steps back of right, pivoting 1/4 left

46-4   Right foot steps back

47-5   Left foot steps back

48-6   Right foot steps back

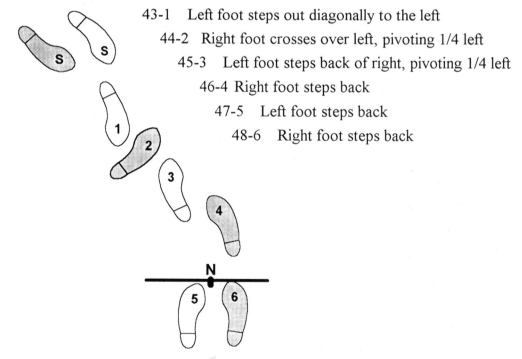

Chapter 5
Moderate Line Dances

BOOT SCOOTIN' BOOGIE

Line dance, moderately easy , 4 walls — 32 counts

Music: "Boot Scootin' Boogie" by Brooks and Dunn

Choreographed by: Tom Mattox and Skippy Blair

Description: Fun dance for warm-up and the song has a nice upbeat tempo. Don't let the name fool you. The BOOT SCOOTIN' BOOGIE does not have any scooting — just slides.

Step, Turn, Step, Turn, Vine Left (1-8 Counts)

1-1   Left foot steps forward

2-2   Turn right 1/2

3-3   Left foot steps forward

4-4   Turn right 1/2

5-1   Left foot steps left

6-2   Right foot steps behind left

7-3   Left foot steps left

8-4   Right foot stomps — Clap

Step, Turn, Step, Turn, Vine Right (9-16 Counts)

9-1   Right foot steps forward

10-2   Turn left 1/2

11-3   Right foot steps forward

12-4   Turn left 1/2

13-1   Right foot steps right

14-2   Left foot steps behind right

15-3   Right foot steps right

16-4   Left foot stomps — Clap

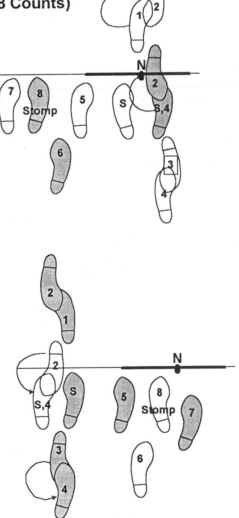

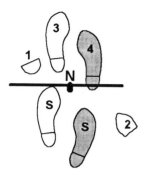

Heel, Toe, Step, Slide (17-20 Counts)

17-1   Left heel touches forward

18-2   Left toe touches on right side of right foot

19-3   Left foot steps forward

20-4   Right foot slides/drags to just behind left foot

Heel, Toe, Step, Slide (21-24 Counts)

21-1   Left heel touches forward

22-2   Left toe touches on right side of right foot

23-3   Left foot steps forward

24-4   Right foot slides/drags to just behind left foot

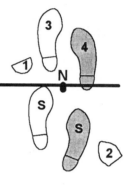

Step, Swivel, Twist, Bump (25-28 Counts)

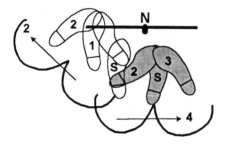

25-1   Left foot steps forward

26-2   Swivel heel left as you bend knees forward pushing hips left

27-3   Twist heels right as you rise, shifting weight right

28-4   Right hip pushes out

Step Turn (29-32 Counts)

29-1   Left foot steps forward

30-2   Right foot steps over left, turning left 1/4

31-3   Left foot steps to right foot

32-4   Pause and clap

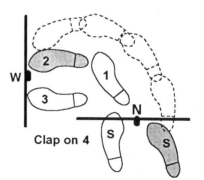

Clap on 4

Note: You also can do a double stomp (left - right or right - left) on the last count of each grapevine. On the boot scoots (counts 17 through 24), some folks lift their left foot, hopping forward on the right foot.

CHOCOLATE CITY HUSTLE

Line dance, moderately easy, 4 walls — 40 counts
Music: "Bop" by Dan Seals, "Norma Jean Riley" by Diamond Rio

Step, Kick (1-4 Counts)

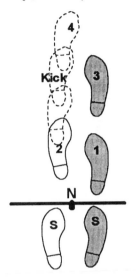

1-1   Right foot steps forward
2-2   Left foot steps forward
3-3   Right foot steps forward
4-4   Left foot kicks forward — Clap

Step Back (5-8 Counts)

5-1   Left foot steps back
6-2   Right foot steps back
7-3   Left foot steps back
8-4   Right toe touches by left foot

Grapevine Right (9-12 Counts)

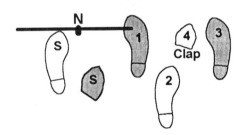

9-1   Right foot steps to right side
10-2   Left foot steps behind right
11-3   Right foot steps right
12-4   Left toe touches by right — Clap

Grapevine Left (13-16 Counts)

13-1   Left foot steps left
14-2   Right foot steps behind left
15-3   Left foot steps left
16-4   Right toe touches by left foot — Clap

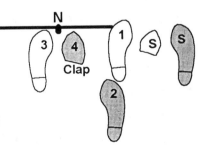

Step, Touch, Step, Touch (17-20 Counts)

17-1   Right foot steps forward — slight angle right

18-2   Left toe touches by right foot — Clap

19-3   Left foot steps back

20-4   Right toe touches by left foot — Clap

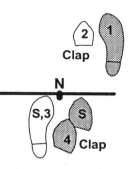

Step, Touch, Step, Touch (21-24 Counts)

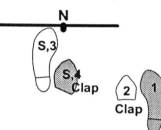

21-1   Right foot steps back — slight angle right

22-2   Left toe touches by right foot — Clap

23-3   Left foot steps left

24-4   Right toe touches by left foot — Clap

Swivel Steps 4Xs (25-32 Counts)

25-1   Right heel and toe step forward and parallel with shoulders

26-2   Right heel swivels 1/4 right

27-3   Left heel and toe step forward and parallel with shoulders

28-4   Left heel swivels 1/4 left

29-1   Right heel and toe step forward and parallel with shoulders

30-6   Right heel swivels 1/4 right

31-7   Left heel and toe step forward and parallel with shoulders

32-8   Left heel swivels 1/4 left

Heel, Heel, Toe, Toe (33-36 Counts)

33-1   Right heel touches forward

34-2   Right heel touches forward

35-3   Right toe touches back

36-4   Right toe touches back

Heel, Toe, Turn (37-40 Counts)

37-1   Right heel touches forward

38-2   Right toe touches back

39-3   Right toe points to right side

40-4   Turn, turning 1/4 right

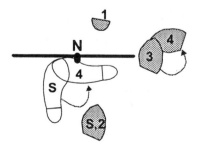

HEY BARTENDER (8 CORNERS or THE EIGHT CORNERS EIGHT COUNT)

Line dance, moderately easy , 4 walls — 40 counts

Music: "Hey Bartender" by Johnny Lee

Description: Popular, easy, good-looking dance. The dance is usually performed in two lines with dancers facing each other. As the dance progresses, the dancers change lines.

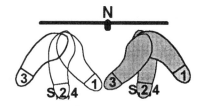

Swivel 4Xs (1-4 Counts)

1-1	Heels swivel right
2-2	Heels swivel back to center
3-3	Heels swivel left
4-4	Heels swivel back to center

Note: Some instructors teach this as a buttermilk instead of swivels.

Point Right, Left (5-12 Counts)

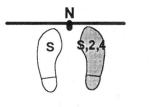

5-1	Right toe touches to right side
6-2	Close — Right foot touches by left foot
7-3	Right toe touches to right side
8-4	Close — Right foot steps by left foot

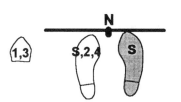

9-1	Left toe touches to left side
10-2	Close — Left foot touches by right foot
11-3	Left toe touches to left side
12-4	Close — Left foot steps by right foot

Heels (13-20 Counts)

13-1	Right heel touches forward
14-2	Close — Right toe touches by left foot
15-3	Right heel touches forward
16-4	Close — Right foot steps by left foot

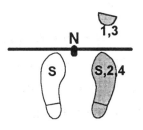

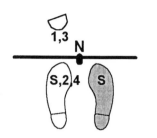

17-1   Left heel touches forward

18-2   Close — Left toe touches by right foot

19-3   Left heel touches forward

20-4   Close — Left foot steps by right foot

Right Boot Hook (21-24 Counts)

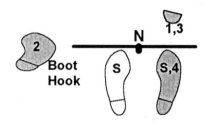

21-1   Right heel touches forward

22-2   Right foot lifts to left knee

23-3   Right heel touches forward

24-4   Close — Right foot steps by left foot

Left Boot Hook (25-28 Counts)

25-1   Left foot touches forward

26-2   Left foot lifts to right knee

27-3   Left foot touches forward

28-4   Left toe touches back by right heel

Charleston 2Xs (29-32 Counts)

29-1   Left foot steps forward

30-2   Right foot kicks forward — Clap

31-3   Right foot steps back

32-4   Left toe touches back

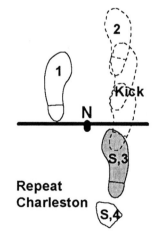

33-1   Left foot steps forward

34-2   Right foot kicks forward — Clap

35-3   Right foot steps back

36-4   Left toe touches back

Note: You can clap the hands for the person in the opposite line.

Step Turn, Step, Step Turn, Stomp (37-40 Counts)

37-1   Left foot steps forward

38-2   Right foot drags to left

39-3   Left foot steps forward, turning 1/4 left

40-4   Right foot stomps by left — Clap

Note: You will change lines with every other series of 40 counts. You move between the dancers in the opposite line on counts 37, 38, and 39.

LONE STAR

Line dance, easy, 4 walls — 32 counts

Music: "I Love a Rainy Night" by Eddie Rabbit

Description: LONE STAR is an easy, lively, line dance that offers a variety of the basic line dancing steps. When you master LONE STAR you are on your way to becoming a pro. Get ready for lots of triple steps.

Heel Touches, Boot Hook (1-4 Counts)

1-1   Right heel out and touches in front

2-2   Right heel turns 1/8 to right and touch

3-3   Right heel turns 1/8 to right and touch

4-4   Right boot hook — Right heel touches left knee

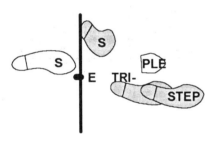

Triple Step (5-6 Counts)

5-1   Right foot steps forward

5-&   Left foot steps forward

6-2   Right foot steps forward

Left Boot Hook (7-8 Counts)

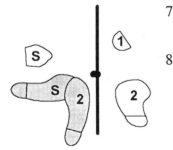

7-1   Left heel forward and touches floor

8-2   Left heel lifts to right knee, turning 1/4 left to begin triple steps

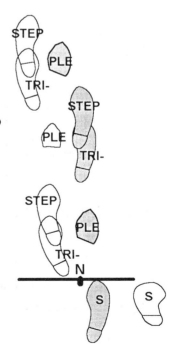

Triple Step 3Xs (9-14 Counts)

9-1   Left triple step — L, R, L — 2 counts

11-3   Right triple step — R, L, R — 2 counts

13-5   Left triple step — L, R, L — 2 counts

Heel, Toe, Triple Step (15-18 Counts)

15-1   Right heel touches forward

16-2   Right toe touches behind left foot

17-3&4   Right triple step — Turn 1/4 right, R, L, R
          — 2 counts

Heel, Hook, Triple Step (19-22 Counts)

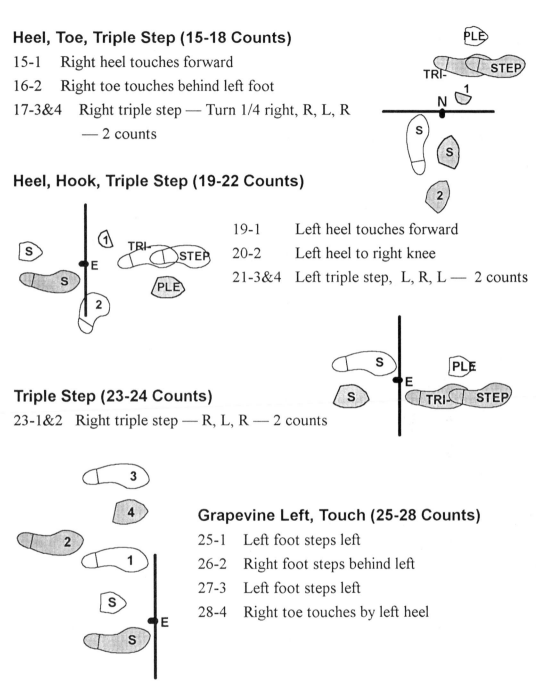

19-1   Left heel touches forward

20-2   Left heel to right knee

21-3&4   Left triple step, L, R, L — 2 counts

Triple Step (23-24 Counts)

23-1&2   Right triple step — R, L, R — 2 counts

Grapevine Left, Touch (25-28 Counts)

25-1   Left foot steps left

26-2   Right foot steps behind left

27-3   Left foot steps left

28-4   Right toe touches by left heel

Heel, Close, Heel, Close (29-32 Counts)

29-1   Right heel touches forward

30-2   Close — Right foot steps back by left foot

31-3   Left heel touches forward

32-4   Close — Left foot steps back by right foot

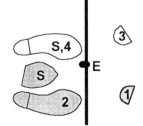

REDNECK GIRL

Line dance, moderate, 4 walls — 36 counts

Music: "Redneck Girl" by the Bellamy Brothers

Description: Lively dance which has withstood the test of time. REDNECK GIRL has been danced for many years.

Buttermilk, Buttermilk (1-4 Counts)

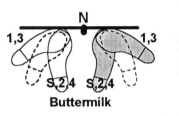

Buttermilk

1-1　Buttermilk — Rise up on toes and spread heels apart

2-2　Close — Lower on toes and heels together

3-3　Buttermilk — Rise up on toes and spread heels apart

4-4　Close — Lower on toes and heels together

Jazz box (5-8 Counts)

5-1　Left foot steps forward

6-2　Right foot crosses over left

7-3　Left foot steps back

8-4　Close — Right foot moves to left foot

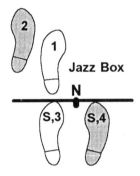

Jazz Box

Jazz Box (9-12 Counts)

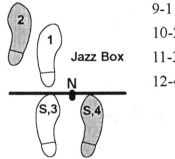

Jazz Box

9-1　Left foot steps forward

10-2　Right foot crosses over left

11-3　Left foot steps back

12-4　Close — Right foot moves to left foot

Heel, Side, Heel, Close (13-16 Counts)

13-1　Left heel touches forward

14-2　Left toe touches left side

15-3　Left heel touches forward

16-4　Close — Left foot steps by right

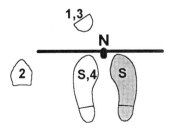

Heel, Side, Heel, Close (17-20 Counts)

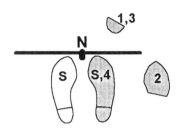

17-1	Right heel touches forward
14-2	Right toe touches right side
15-3	Right heel touches forward
16-4	Close — Right foot steps by left

Heel, Toe, Triple Step (21-24 Counts)

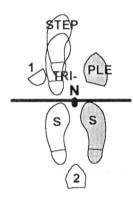

21-1	Left heel touches forward
22-2	Left toe touches back
23-3	Left foot steps forward
23-&	Right foot steps forward
24-4	Left foot steps forward

Heel, Toe, Triple Step 2Xs (25-30 Counts)

25-1	Right heel touches forward
26-2	Right toe touches back
27-3	Right foot steps forward
27-&	Left foot steps forward
28-4	Right foot steps forward
29-5	Left foot steps forward
29-&	Right foot steps forward
30-6	Left foot steps forward

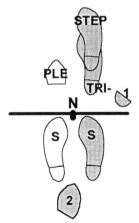

Turn Triple Step (31-32 Counts)

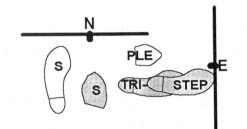

31-1   Right foot steps 1/4 turning right

31-&   Left foot steps forward

32-2   Right foot steps forward

Back, Back, Back, Stomp (33-36 Counts)

33-1   Left foot steps back

34-2   Right foot steps back

35-3   Left foot steps back

36-4   Right foot stomps — Clap

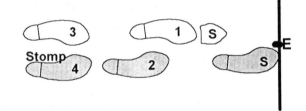

T. C. ELECTRIC SLIDE

Line dance, moderate, 4 walls — 30 counts

Music: "Some Kind of Trouble" by Tanya Tucker, "Electric Slide" by M.C. Hammer, "Stroking" by Clarence Carter, "Blue To The Bone" by Sweethearts Of The Rodeo

Description: T.C. ELECTRIC SLIDE, as you can imagine, is a variation of the ELECTRIC SLIDE. The T.C. ELECTRIC SLIDE is more difficult than the ELECTRIC SLIDE or the WESTERN ELECTRIC SLIDE. The T.C. ELECTRIC SLIDE and the WESTERN ELECTRIC SLIDE follow the beats of the music; whereas the ELECTRIC SLIDE in some places, does not. Also, the other two slides add a level of difficulty to the dance, contributing to the challenge and fun. It is very common to find the ELECTRIC SLIDE and THE T.C. ELECTRIC SLIDE sharing the different halves of the floor.

Step, Slide, Step, Slide, Step, Touch (1-4 Counts)

1-1   Right foot steps to the right side

1-&   Left foot slides to right foot

2-2   Right foot steps right

2-&   Left foot slides to right foot

3-3   Right foot steps right

4-4   Left toe touches by right foot

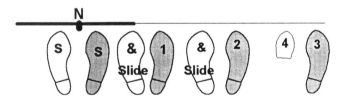

Step, Slide, Step, Slide, Step, Touch (5-8 counts)

5-1   Left foot steps left

5-&   Right foot slides left

6-2   Left foot steps left

6-&   Right foot slides left

7-3   Left foot steps left

8-4   Right toe touches by left

Walk Back (9-12 Counts)

9-1   Right foot steps back

10-2   Left foot steps back

11-3   Right foot steps back

12-4   Stomp left foot — Clap is optional

Jump Steps — Out, Out, In, In (13-14 Counts)

13-&   Left foot steps left — Out

13-1   Right foot steps right — Out

14-&   Left foot steps to center — In

14-2   Right foot steps to center — In

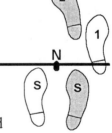

Note: Take small short quick steps — 4 steps in 2 counts/beats. It helps to stay on the balls (forward part) of your feet. If one has difficulty with doing this modified jumping jack, do a W-A-T-C-H-O-U-T or a buttermilk.

Step, Step (15-16 Counts)

15-1   Left foot steps across in front of right

16-2   Right foot crosses in front of left

Step, Rock, Rock, Slide (17-20 Counts)

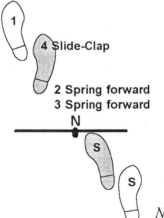

17-1   Left foot steps forward and to the left—Step 1/8 left taking a large step

18-2   Left foot rocks or bounces forward — Springing with left knee

19-3   Left foot rocks or bounces forward — Springing with left knee

20-4   Right foot slides to left while left is turning 1/8 left — Clap

Note: Shoulder shimmies are optional on counts 2 and 3.

Step, Rock, Rock, Slide (21-24 Counts)

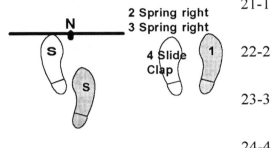

21-1	Right foot steps right — Taking a large step
22-2	Rock or bounce right — Springing with right knee
23-3	Rock or bounce right — Springing with right knee
24-4	Left foot slides to right — Clap

Note: Shoulder shimmies are optional on counts 2 & 3.

Hip Bumps (25-28 Counts)

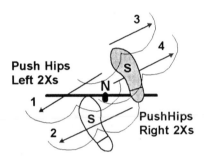

25-1	Rock hips left
26-2	Rock hips left
27-3	Rock hips right
28-4	Rock hips right

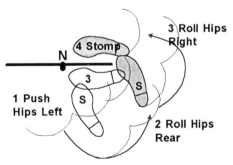

Roll Hips, Stomp (29-32 Counts)

29-1 Rock hips left

30-2 Roll hips front to rear

31-3 Roll hips rear to front, turning 1/4 left on left foot

32-4 Right foot stomps by left — Clap

Note: Bend the knees while rolling the hips, making a smooth circle. The hips will roll a little more than 1/2 of a circle. Some dancers take a deep breath before starting this hip roll, yelling out W-H-O-O-O-O-O-P until the roll is completed.

WILD WILD WEST

Line dance, moderately easy but fast, 2 walls — 24 counts

Music: any fast Cha-Cha, "Wild Wild West" by The Escape Club, "I Had a Beautiful Time" by Merle Haggard

Description: Very aerobic, fast CHA-CHA. If you want a real workout, this is the line dance to do that, especially with the Escape Club's "Wild Wild West".

Left Triple Step, Rock, Step (1-4 Counts)

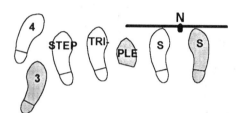

1-1	Left foot steps left
1-&	Right toe steps by left foot
2-2	Left foot steps left
3-3	Right foot rocks back
4-4	Left foot steps forward

Right Triple Step, Rock, Step (5-8 Counts)

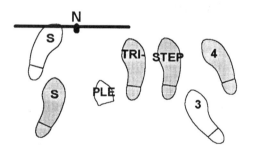

5-1	Right foot steps right
5-&	Left toe steps by right foot
6-2	Right foot steps right
7-3	Left foot rocks back
8-4	Right foot steps forward

Turning Triple Step, Rock, Step (9-12 Counts)

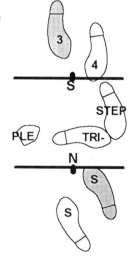

9-1 Left foot steps forward, turning 1/4 right

9-& Right toe steps by left foot

10-2 Left foot steps back, turning 1/4 right

11-3 Right foot rocks back

12-4 Left foot steps forward

Turning Triple Step, Rock, Step (13-16 Counts)

13-1   Right foot steps forward, turning 1/4 left

13-&   Left toe steps by right foot

14-2   Right foot steps back, turning 1/4 left

15-3   Left foot rocks back

16-4   Right foot steps forward

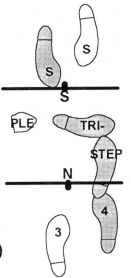

Left Triple Step, Right Triple Step (17-20 Counts)

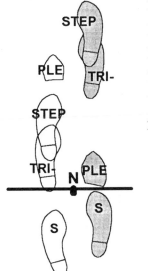

17-1   Left foot steps forward

17-&   Right toe steps by left foot

18-2   Left foot steps forward

19-3   Right foot steps forward

19-&   Left toe steps by right foot

20-2   Right foot steps forward

Grapevine Left, Turn (20-24 Counts)

21-1   Left foot steps left

22-2   Right foot steps behind left foot

23-3   Left foot steps left, turning 1/2 right

24-4   Right foot stomps by left — End with weight on right foot

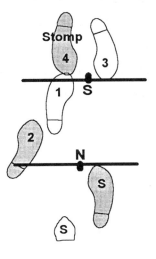

Chapter 6
Intermediate Line Dances

6-STEP, SIX (COUNT) STEP

Line dance, moderate, 4 walls — 40 counts

Music: "Norma Jean Riley" by Diamond Rio

Description: The number of steps makes this dance a little difficult, but it is a fun series of steps.

Heel, Close, Heel, Close (1-4 Counts)

1-1   Right heel touches forward

2-2   Close — Right foot back to center

3-3   Right heel touches forward

4-4   Close — Right foot back to center

Heel, Close, Heel, Close (5-8 Counts)

5-1   Left heel touches forward

6-2   Close — Left foot back to center

7-3   Left heel touches forward

8-4   Close — Left foot back to center

Heel, Close, Heel, Boot Hook (9-12 Counts)

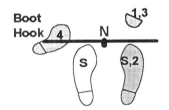

9-1   Right heel touches forward

10-2   Close — Right foot back to center

11-3   Right heel touches forward

12-4   Right boot hook — Right foot lifts to left knee

Heel, Close, Watch-Out (13-16 Counts)

13-1   Right heel touches forward

14-2   Close — Right foot back to center

15-3   Both feet jump out — Say "WATCH"

16-4   Both feet jump together — Say "OUT"

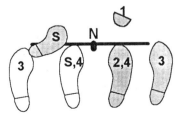

Note: If you prefer, do a buttermilk instead of a jumping-jack. It's easier on the body.

Heel, Close, Heel, Boot Hook (17-20 Counts)

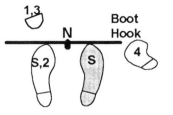

17-1 Left heel touches forward

18-2 Close — Left foot back to center

19-3 Left heel touches forward

20-4 Left boot hook — Left foot lift to right knee

Heel, Toe, Step, Scoot (21-24 Counts)

21-1   Left heel touches forward

22-2   Left toe touches by right heel

23-3   Left foot steps forward

24-4   Left foot scoots forward and clap

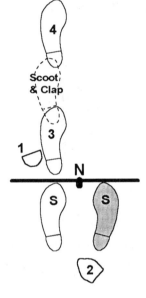

Step, Scoot, Step, Scoot (25-28 Counts)

25-1   Right foot steps right

26-2   Right foot drags back, turning 1/4 right and clap

27-3   Left foot steps forward

28-4   Left foot scoots forward and clap

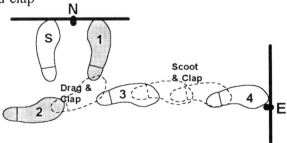

Step, Step, Step, Stomp (29-32 Counts)

29-1 Right foot steps back

30-2 Left foot steps back

31-3 Right foot steps back

32-4 Left foot stomps by right

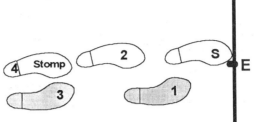

Toe, Scuff, Heel, Close (33-36 Counts)

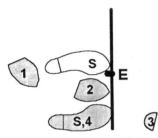

33-1 Right toe touches behind

34-2 Right toe touches to center — Scuff foot for accent

35-3 Right heel touches forward

36-4 Close — Right foot to center

Swivel 4Xs (37-40 Counts)

37-1 Swivel right — Both heels

38-2 Swivel left — Heels back to center

39-3 Swivel left — Both heels

40-4 Swivel right — Heels back to center

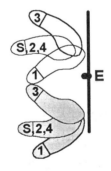

COPPERHEAD ROAD

Line dance, easy to moderate, 4 walls — 22 counts

Music: "Copperhead Road" by Steve Earle, "Rock My Baby Tonight" by Mighty Joe Young, "Queen Of Memphis" by Confederate Railroad

Description: Aerobic dance with side hop. Get ready for a real workout!

Heel, Close, Toe, Close (1-4 Counts)

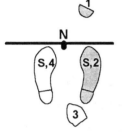

1-1 Right heel touches forward

2-2 Close — Right foot steps by left

3-3 Left toe touches behind right foot

4-4 Close — Left foot steps by right

Touch, Vine Right and Turn (5-8 Counts)

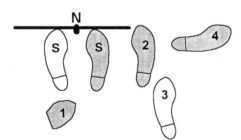

5-1 Right toe touches behind left foot

6-2 Right foot steps right

7-3 Left foot steps behind right

8-4 Right foot steps right, turning 1/4 right

Hop, Hop, Step, Slap (9-12 Counts)

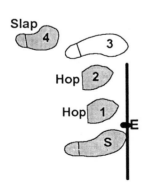

9-1 Right foot hops left — Lift left leg with knee bent

10-2 Right foot hops left

11-3 Left foot steps left

12-4 Right foot lifts behind left knee, slap leather (slap right boot with left hand)

Vine Right, Slap (13-16 Counts)

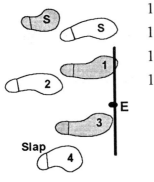

13-1	Right foot steps right
14-2	Left foot steps behind right
15-3	Right foot steps right
16-4	Left foot lifts behind right knee, slap leather (slap left boot with right hand).

Back, Back, Back, Hop (17-20 Counts)

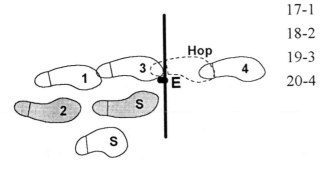

17-1	Left foot steps back
18-2	Right foot steps back
19-3	Left foot steps forward
20-4	Left foot hops forward — Hitch right foot

Stomp, Stomp (21-22 Counts)

21-1	Right foot stomps
22-2	Left foot stomps

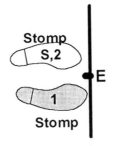

SLAPPIN' LEATHER

Line dance: moderately easy, 4 walls — 40 counts

Music: "Back Roads" by Ricky Van Shelton, "Stand Up" by Mel McDaniel

Description: Very lively dance. Swinging the right foot from the back to the side, from the side to the front, from the front to the side is an interesting move. Don't let the move fool you. It is not that difficult. Like so many other line dances, SLAPPIN' LEATHER has many versions. Knowing one, you will have no difficulty joining a group with a slightly different version. In some areas, the dance is started with the buttermilk. Your choice!

Heel, Close, Heel, Close (1-4 Counts)

1-1 Right heel touches forward

2-2 Close — Right foot steps by left

3-3 Left heel touches forward

4-4 Close — Left foot steps by right

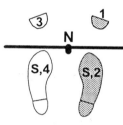

Heel, Close, Heel, Close (5-8 Counts)

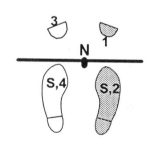

5-1 Right heel touches forward

6-2 Close — Right foot steps by left

7-3 Left heel touches forward

8-4 Close — Left foot steps by right

Heel, Heel, Toe, Toe (9-12 Counts)

9-1 Right heel touches forward

10-2 Right heel touches forward

11-3 Right toe touches back

12-4 Right toe touches back

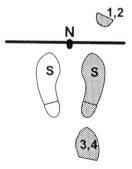

Heel, Toe, Toe, Toe, Slap, Slap, Slap, Slap (13-20 Counts)

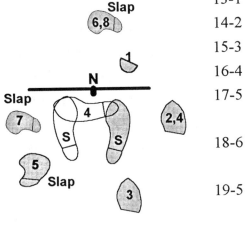

13-1	Right heel touches forward
14-2	Right toe touches right side
15-3	Right toe touches back
16-4	Right toe touches right side
17-5	Right foot swings back of left knee, slap with left hand
18-6	Right foot swings out to right side, slap with right hand, turning 1/4 left
19-5	Right foot swings in front of left knee, slap with left hand
20-6	Right foot swings out to right side, slap with right hand

Note: Some instructors delete the third and fourth toe touches.

Vine Right (21-24 counts)

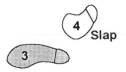

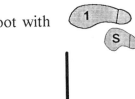

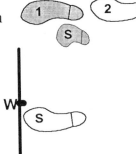

21-1   Right foot steps to the right

22-2   Left foot steps behind right

23-3   Right foot steps right

24-4   Left foot lifts behind right knee, slap boot with right hand

Vine Left (25-28 Counts)

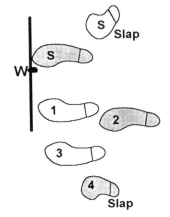

25-1   Left foot steps left

26-2   Right foot steps behind left

27-3   Left foot steps left

28-4   Right foot lifts behind left knee, slap boot with left hand

Step, Step, Step Scoot (29-32 Counts)

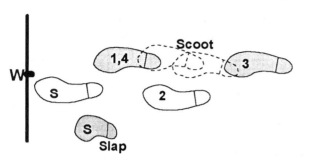

29-1	Right foot steps back
30-2	Left foot steps back
31-3	Right foot steps back
32-4	Right foot scoots forward

Step, Drag, Step, Stomp (33-36 Counts)

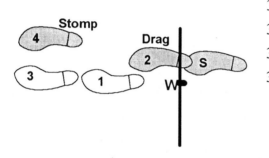

33-1	Left foot steps forward
34-2	Right foot drags to left
35-3	Left foot steps forward
36-4	Right foot stomps by left

Swivel 4Xs (37-40 Counts)

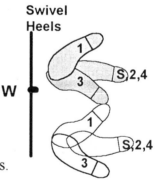

37-1	Swivel heels right
38-2	Swivel heels left
39-3	Swivel heels left
40-4	Swivel heels right

Note: The swivels can be replaced with buttermilks.

SOUTH SIDE SHUFFLE

Line dance, intermediate, 2 walls — 28 counts

Music: "Stand Up" by Mel McDaniel, "Back Roads" by Ricky Van Shelton, "Hillbilly Rock" by Marty Stuart, "When Twist Comes to Shout" by Sawyer Brown

Fan Right 2Xs (1-4 Counts)

1-1   Right toe swivels to right

2-2   Right toe back to front

3-3   Right toe swivels to right

4-4   Right toe back to front

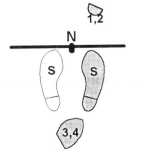

Heel, Heel, Toe, Toe (5-8 Counts)

5-1   Right heel touches forward

6-2   Right heel touches forward

7-3   Right toe touches behind left foot

8-4   Right toe touches behind left foot

Heel, Toe, Side, Back (9-12 Counts)

9-1   Right heel touches forward

10-2   Right toe touches left heel

11-3   Right toe touches to right side

12-4   Right toe touches behind left heel

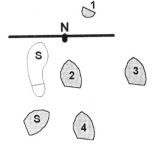

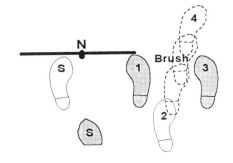

Grapevine Right, Brush (13-16 Counts)

13-1   Right foot steps right

14-2   Left foot steps behind right

15-3   Right foot steps right

16-4   Left foot brushes by right

Grapevine Left, Brush (17-20 Counts)

17-1   Left foot steps left

18-2   Right foot steps behind left

19-3   Left foot steps left

20-4   Right foot brushes by left

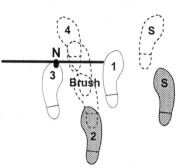

Step, Step Together, Step, Brush (21-24 Counts)

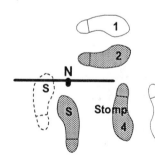

21-1   Right foot steps forward

22-2   Left foot steps forward to right foot

23-3   Right foot steps forward

24-4   Left foot brushes by right

Turn, Step, Turn, Stomp (25-28 Counts)

25-1   Left foot steps forward, turning 1/4 right

26-2   Right foot steps by left

27-3   Left foot steps forward, turning 1/4 right

28-4   Right foot stomps by left

TAHOE TWIST

Line dance, moderately easy, 4 walls — 36 counts

Music: "The Fireman" by George Strait, "T For Texas" by Waylon Jennings, "Two More Bottles of Wine" by Emmylou Harris, "Headed For A Heartache" by Gary Morris

Description: One of the older line dances; still unique and enjoyable.

Heel, Close, Heel, Close (1-4 Counts)

1-1   Right heel touches forward

2-2   Close — Right foot steps by left

3-3   Left heel touches forward

4-4   Close — Left foot steps by right

Buttermilk, Buttermilk (5-8 Counts)

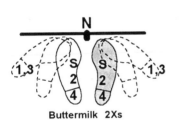

Buttermilk 2Xs

5-1   Heels out — Weight on toes, move both heels to the outside

6-2   Move heels back together

7-3   Heels out — Weight on toes, move both heels to the outside

8-4   Move heels back together

Right Boot Hook (9-12 Counts)

9-1   Right heel touches forward

10-2   Right heel touches left knee

11-3   Right heel touches front

12-4   Close — Right foot steps by left

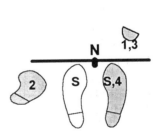

Left Boot Hook (13-16 Counts)

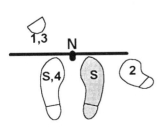

13-1   Left heel touches forward

14-2   Left heel touches right knee

15-3   Left heel touches forward

16-4   Close — Left foot steps by right

Swivel, Twist, Twist, Swivel (17-20 Counts)

17-1   Swivel heels to the left

18-2   Twist heels to the right

19-3   Twist heels to the left

20-4   Swivel heels to the center — Keep feet together

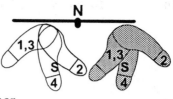

Heel, Slap, Heel, Close (21-24 Counts)

21-1   Right heel touches forward

22-2   Right foot crosses back of left leg and
        slap boot with left hand

23-3   Right heel touches forward

24-4   Close — Right foot steps by left

Heel, Slap, Heel, Touch (25-28 Counts)

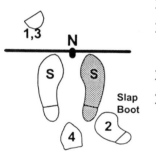

25-1   Left heel touches forward

26-2   Left foot crosses back of right leg and slap boot
        with right hand

27-3   Left heel touches forward

28-4   Left toe touches back

Step, Kick, Step, Turn (29-32 Counts)

29-1   Left foot steps forward

30-2   Right foot kicks forward

31-3   Right foot steps back

32-4   Right foot hops forward, turning 1/4
        left — Left knee lifts

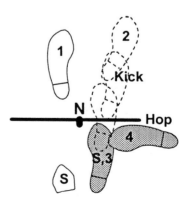

Vine Left, Stomp (33-36 Counts)

33-1	Left foot steps to left side
34-2	Right foot steps behind left foot
35-3	Left foot steps to left side
36-4	Right foot stomps by left foot

TULSA TIME

Line dance, intermediate, 4 walls — 64 counts

Music: "Tulsa Time" by Don Williams

Description: The number of steps makes the dance difficult. TULSA TIME is one of those dances for which it seems only appropriate to use its namesake music, "Tulsa Time".

Sleek Side Steps (1-4 Counts)

1-1   Left foot steps left

2-2   Right foot slides to left

3-3   Left foot steps left

4-4   Right foot slides to left

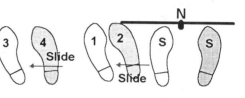

Sleek Side Steps (5-8 Counts)

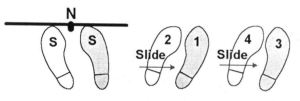

5-1   Right foot steps right

6-2   Left foot slides to right

7-3   Right foot steps right

8-4   Left foot slides to right

Sleek Side Steps (9-12 Counts)

9-1   Left foot steps left

10-2   Right foot slides to left

11-3   Left foot steps left

12-4   Right foot slides to left

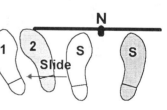
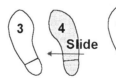

Sleek Side Steps (13-16 Counts)

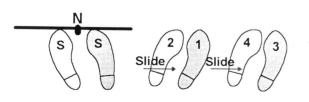

13-1   Right foot steps right

14-2   Left foot slides to right

15-3   Right foot steps right

16-4   Left foot slides to right

Two Charleston Steps (17-24 Counts)

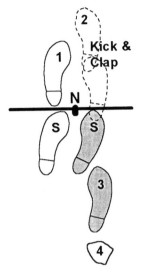

17-1	Left foot steps forward
18-2	Right foot kicks forward and clap hands
19-3	Right foot steps back
20-4	Left toe touches behind right heel
21-5	Left foot steps forward
12-6	Right foot kicks forward and clap hands
23-7	Right foot steps back
24-8	Left toe touches behind right heel

Vine Left And Kick (25-28 Counts)

25-1	Left foot steps left
26-2	Right foot steps behind left
27-3	Left foot steps left
28-4	Right foot scuffs or kicks forward and clap hands

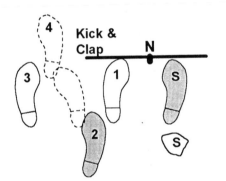

Vine Right And Kick (29-32 Counts)

29-1	Right foot steps right
30-2	Left foot steps behind right
31-3	Right foot steps right
32-4	Left foot brushes or kicks forward — Clap

Step And Kick 6Xs (33-44 Counts)

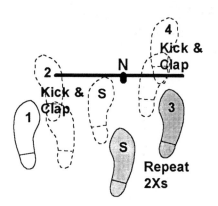

33-1	Left foot steps left
34-2	Right foot kicks forward — Clap
35-3	Right foot steps right
36-4	Left foot kicks forward — Clap
37-1	Left foot steps left
38-2	Right foot kicks forward — Clap
39-3	Right foot steps right
40-4	Left foot kicks forward — Clap

41-1	Left foot steps left
42-2	Right foot kicks forward — Clap
43-3	Right foot steps right
44-4	Left foot kicks forward — Clap

Step, Stomp, Click, Click (45-48 Counts)

45-1	Left foot takes large step left
46-2	Right foot stomps by left foot
47-3	Click heels together
48-4	Click heels together

Step, Close, Step, Turn (49-52 Counts)

49-1	Left foot steps forward
50-2	Close — Right foot steps by left
51-3	Left foot steps forward
52-4	Turn on left foot, turning 1/2 right

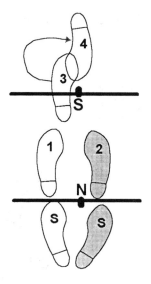

Step, Close, Step, Turn (53-56 Counts)

53-1   Right foot steps forward

54-2   Close — Left foot steps by right

55-3   Right foot steps forward

56-4   Turn on right foot, turning 1/2 left

Left Triple Step, Right Triple Step (57-60 Counts)

57-1   Left foot steps forward

57-&   Right foot steps forward

58-2   Left foot steps forward

59-3   Right foot steps forward

59-&   Left foot steps forward

60-4   Right foot steps forward

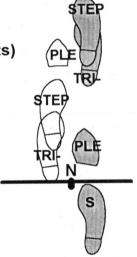

Step, Crossover, Step, Close (61-64 Counts)

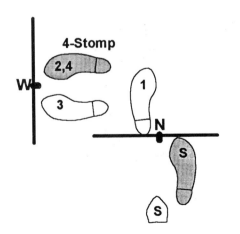

61-1   Left foot steps forward

62-2   Right foot crosses over left, turning
        left 1/4

63-3   Left foot steps by right

64-4   Right foot stomps by left

WALKIN' WAZI

Line dance, intermediate, 2 walls — 40 counts

Music: "Tear Stained Letter" by Jo-El Sonnier, "Dumas Walker" by Kentucky Head-hunters, "We'll Burn That Bridge" by Brooks & Dunn

Description: The toe-heel movements and the double grapevines (traveling grape-vine) add some very interesting movements to this dance. Also, the double grape-vines cover a lot of dance floor, even when you take small steps. This is definitely one of those dances that is difficult or impossible to do on a crowded dance floor.

    Kelly Gellette, one of the foremost historians and instructors of country western dancing, tells the story of a man named Wazi, who showed a little dance movement to his friend, George. George liked the dance and showed it to his friend, Dave Getty. Dave added some extra steps and came up with a 4-wall dance called WALKIN' WAZI. This 2-wall version is very similar to the 4 wall version except for the number of turns. It's easier to do and doesn't require as much hardwood.

Toe, Heel, Toe, Heel (1-4 Counts)

1-1 Right toe touches forward — Slightly

2-2 Right heel steps down

3-3 Left toe touches forward — Slightly

4-4 Left heel steps down

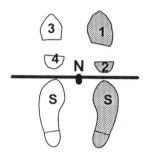

Kick, Touch (5-8 Counts)

5-1 Right foot kicks forward — Keep foot off floor

6-2 Right foot kicks forward

7-3 Right foot steps back

8-4 Left toe touches by right heel

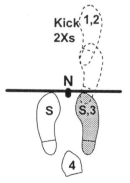

Step, Brush, Toe, Heel (9-10 Counts)

9-1   Left foot steps forward

10-2 Right foot brushes left foot, turning 1/4 left

Toe, Heel, Toe, Heel (11-14 Counts)

11-1   Right toe touches forward — Slightly

12-2   Right heel steps down

13-3   Left toe touches forward — Slightly

14-4   Left heel steps down

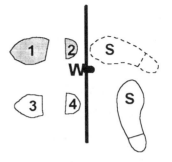

Kick, Touch (15-18 Counts)

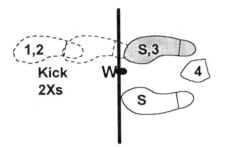

15-1   Right foot kicks forward — Keep foot off floor

16-2   Right foot kicks forward

17-3   Right foot steps back

18-4   Left toe touches by right heel

Step, Turn (19-20 Counts)

19-1   Left foot steps forward

20-2   Right foot brushes left foot, turning 1/4 left

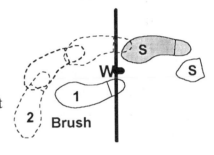

Traveling Grapevine — Double Vine Right (21-28 Counts)

21-1   Right foot steps right

22-2   Left foot steps behind right

23-3   Right foot steps right

24-4   Left foot steps across (in front of) right

25-5   Right foot steps right

26-6   Left foot steps behind right

27-7   Right foot steps right

28-8   Left foot steps across right

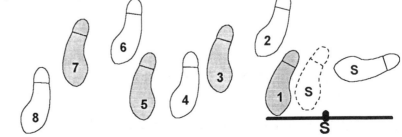

Turn, Step, Rock, Rock (29-32 Counts)

29-1   Right foot swings turning 1/4 left

30-2   Right foot steps down

31-3   Left foot rocks back

32-4   Right foot rocks forward

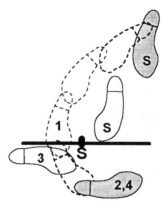

Step, Push, Step, Push (33-36 Counts)

33-1   Left foot steps forward

34-2   Left foot pushes, turning 1/4 right, right foot turns

35-3   Left foot steps forward

36-4   Left foot pushes, turning 1/2 right, right foot turns

Step, Push, Stomp, Stomp (37-40 Counts)

37-1   Left foot steps forward

38-2   Left foot pushes, turning 1/2 right, right foot turns

39-3   Left foot stomps by right

40-4   Left foot stomps

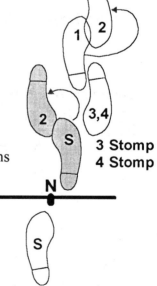

Chapter 7
Expert Line Dances

COUNTRY STRUT

Line dance, moderately difficult, 4 walls — 36 counts

Music: "Some Kind of Trouble" by Tanya Tucker, "She's an Old Cadillac" by Eddie Rabbit, "Round the Clock Lovin'" by K.T. Oslin

Description: The dance has an interesting variation to the boot hook. It is an outside type of boot hook or kick out.

Heel, Hook, Heel, Kick, Heel, Close (1-6 Counts)

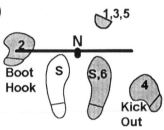

1-1 Right heel touches forward

2-2 Right foot lifts to left knee

3-3 Right heel touches forward

4-4 Right foot — Swing and kick heel out to right side

5-5 Right heel touches forward

6-6 Close — Right foot steps by left

Heel, Hook, Heel, Kick, Heel, Close (7-12 Counts)

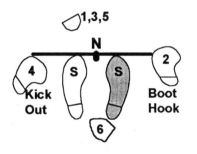

7-1 Left heel touches forward

8-2 Left foot lifts to right knee

9-3 Left heel touches forward

10-4 Left foot — Swing and kick heel out to left side

11-5 Left heel touches forward

12-6 Left toe touches back

Charleston (13-16 Counts)

13-1 Left foot steps forward

14-2 Right foot kicks forward and clap

15-3 Right foot steps back

16-4 Left toe touches back

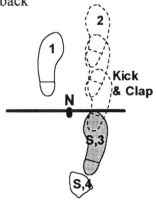

Step, Drag, Step, Turn (17-20 Counts)

17-1   Left foot steps forward

18-2   Right foot drags to left foot

19-3   Left foot steps forward

20-4   Right foot swings over left, turning left 1/2 (leave weight on left foot)

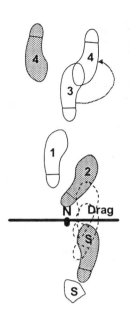

Duck Slap Steps — Struts (21-28 Counts)

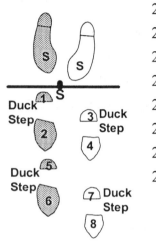

21-1   Right heel touches forward

22-2   Right toe slaps floor

23-3   Left heel touches forward

24-4   Left toe slaps floor

25-5   Right heel touches forward

26-6   Right toe slaps floor

27-7   Left heel touches forward

28-8   Left toe slaps forward

Jazz Box (29-32 Counts)

29-1   Right foot crosses over left

30-2   Left foot steps back

31-3   Right foot steps right, turning right 1/4

32-4   Close — Left foot steps by right

Jazz Box (33-36 Counts)

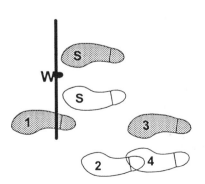

33-1   Right foot crosses over left

34-2   Left foot steps back

35-3   Right foot steps back

36-4   Close — Left foot steps by right

DUKE

Line dance, easy expert, 4 walls — 36 counts

Music: "Heartland" by George Strait

Description: Exciting fast dance, easier than COUNTRY STRUT. The music allows you a few bars to run to the floor. Start dancing when George begins to sing. As always, clapping with a stomp or touch is optional, but it is surprising how a clap will help with your timing.

Grapevine Right (1-4 Counts)

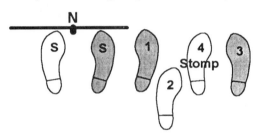

1-1   Right foot steps right

2-2   Left foot steps behind right

3-3   Right foot steps right

4-4   Left foot stomps by right — Clap

Grapevine Left (5-8 Counts)

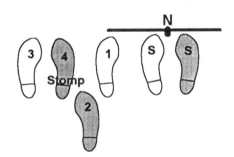

5-1   Left foot steps left

6-2   Right foot steps behind left foot

7-3   Left foot steps left

8-4   Right foot stomps by left — Clap

Walk Back (9-12 Counts)

9-1   Right foot steps back

10-2   Left foot steps back

11-3   Right foot steps back

12-4   Left toe touches by right — Clap

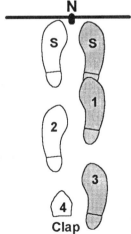

Left Triple Step, Right Triple Step, Left Triple Step (13-18 Counts)

13-1   Left foot steps forward

13-&   Right toe touches forward

14-2   Left foot steps forward

15-3   Right foot steps forward

15-&   Left toe touches forward

16-4   Right foot steps forward

17-1   Left foot steps forward

17-&   Right toe touches forward

18-2   Left foot steps forward

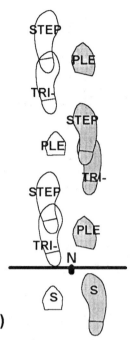

Heel, Heel, Toe, Toe, Heel, Touch (19-24 Counts)

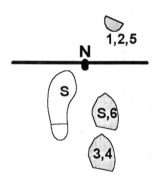

19-1   Right heel touches front

20-2   Right heel touches front

21-3   Right toe touches back

22-4   Right toe touches back

23-5   Right heel touches front

24-6   Right toe touches by left foot

Touch, Slap, Touch, Slap (25-28 Counts)

25-1   Right toe touches to right side

26-2   Right foot swings up in front of left knee and slap with left hand

27-3   Right toe touches to right side

28-4   Right foot swings up in front of left knee and slap with left hand

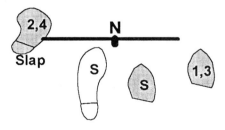

Turn, Slap (29-30 COUNTS)

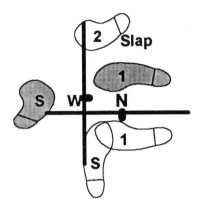

29-1   Left foot turns 1/4 left, right foot steps by left

30-2   Left foot swings up in front of right knee — Slap with right hand

6-Count Grapevine Left (31-36 counts)

31-1   Left foot steps down by right heel

32-2   Right foot steps across in front of left foot

33-3   Left foot steps left

34-4   Right foot steps behind left foot

35-5   Left foot steps left

36-6   Right foot stomps by left — Clap

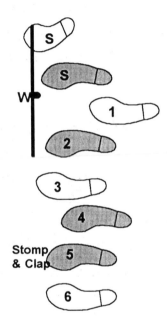

GET RHYTHM

Line dance, easy expert, 4 walls — 36 counts

Music: "Get Rhythm" by Norton Del Ray, "Get Rhythm" by Johnny Cash

Description: GET RHYTHM has a nice swing feel. The difficult steps are the rocking steps with turns.

Crossing Triple Step 3Xs (1-8 Counts)

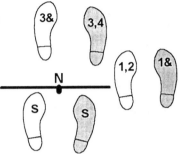

1-1   Left foot crosses over right foot

1-&   Right foot steps by left

2-2   Left foot steps in place

3-3   Right foot crosses over left

3-&   Left foot steps by right

4-4   Right foot steps in place

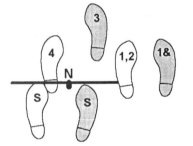

5-1   Left foot crosses over right

5-&   Right foot steps by left

6-2   Left foot steps in place

7-3   Right foot crosses over left

8-4   Left foot steps back

Step, Cross, Turns, Stomp (9-14 Counts)

9-1   Right foot steps right slightly, turning 1/4 right

10-2   Left foot crosses right

         Note: Begin left $360°$ pivot

11-3   Right foot steps back, turning 1/4 left

12-4   Left foot steps left, turning 1/2 left

13-5   Right foot steps right, turning 1/4 left

14-6   Left foot stomps by right

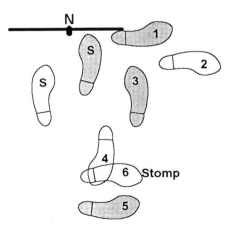

Kick-Ball Change, Step, Drag (15-18 Counts)

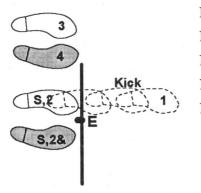

15-1   Left foot kicks forward

16-2   Left foot steps by right

16-&   Right foot steps in place

17-3   Left foot steps left

18-4   Right foot drags to left

Kick-Ball Change, Step, Drag (19-22 Counts)

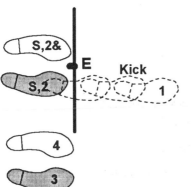

19-1   Right foot kicks forward

20-2   Right foot steps by left

20-&   Left foot steps in place

21-3   Right foot steps right

22-4   Left foot drags to right

Charleston (23-26 Counts)

23-1   Left toe touches back

24-2   Left foot steps forward

25-3   Right foot kicks forward

26-4   Right foot steps back

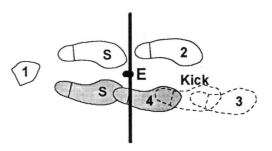

Toe, Step, Drag, Step (27-30 Counts)

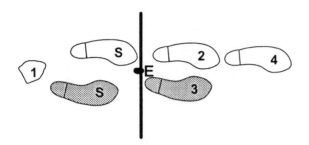

27-1 Left toe touches back

28-2 Left foot steps forward

29-3 Right foot drags to left

30-4 Left foot steps forward

Kick, Crossover, Step, Step, Toe, Toe (31-36 Counts)

31-1 Right foot kicks forward

32-2 Right foot steps over left

33-3 Left foot steps back

34-4 Right foot steps back

35-5 Left toe touches back

36-6 Left toe touches to left side

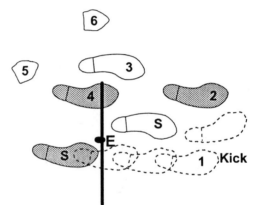

LE DOUX SHUFFLE

Line dance, expert, 4 walls — 96 counts

Music: "Cadillac Ranch" by Chris Le Doux or any TUSH PUSH song

Description: If you have THE TUSH PUSH down pat, the LE DOUX SHUFFLE will be a snap. The Le Doux Shuffle is an 18-step sequence that is a basic part of THE TUSH PUSH.

Right Boot Hook (1-4 Counts)

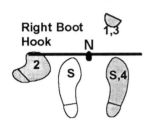

1-1	Right heel touches forward
2-2	Right heel lifts to left knee
3-3	Right heel touches forward
4-4	Close — Right foot steps by left

Left Boot Hook (5-8 Counts)

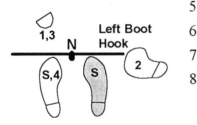

5-1	Left heel touches forward
6-2	Left heel lifts to right knee
7-3	Left heel touches forward
8-4	Close — Left foot steps by right

Right Boot Hook (9-12 Counts)

9-1   Right heel touches forward

10-2   Right heel lifts to left knee

11-3   Right heel touches forward

12-4   Right toe touches back

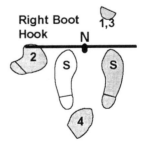

13-30 Le Doux Shuffle*

Note: You will find the 18-step Le Doux Shuffle at the end (page 124).

Stomp, Clap, Heel (31-36 Counts)

31-1   Right foot stomps by left

32-2   Hold — Clap

33-3   Right heel touches forward and tap toe

34-4   Tap toe

35-5   Tap toe

36-6   Tap toe

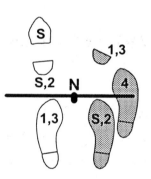

Hop, Heel (37-40 Counts)

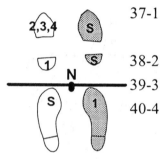

37-1   Hop with left heel touching forward, and right foot back — tap toe

38-2   Tap toe

39-3   Tap toe

40-4   Tap toe

Hops (41-44 Counts)

41-1   Hop — Left foot back to close and right heel touches forward

42-2   Hop — Right foot back to close and left heel touches forward

43-3   Hop — Left foot back to close and right heel touches forward

44-4   Right foot slides back and clap (shift weight to right foot)

Push Tush -- 2 To The Front & 2 To The Rear (45-48 Counts)

45-1   Rock hips forward

46-2   Rock hips forward

47-3   Rock hips to rear

48-4   Rock hips to rear

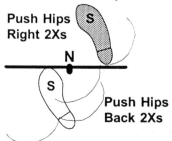

Push Tush -- Front, Rear, Front, Rear (49-52 Counts)

49-1   Rock hips forward

50-2   Rock hips back

51-3   Rock hips forward

52-4   Rock hips back

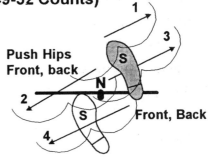

53-70 Le Doux Shuffle*

Stomp, Jumping-Jacks, Turn (71-74 Counts)

71-1   Right foot stomps by left

72-2   Jump, both feet apart

73-3   Jump, right foot over left — Feet change positions

74-4   Turn 1/2 left

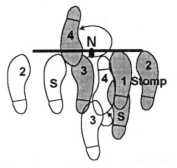

75-92 Le Doux Shuffle*

Jazz Box (93-96 Counts)

93-1   Right foot steps across left, turning 1/4 left

94-2   Left foot steps back

95-3   Right foot steps right

96-4   Left foot stomps by right — Clap

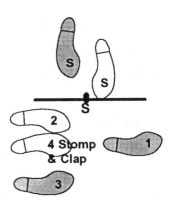

*START — Le Doux Shuffle (18 Counts)

Right Triple Step, Step, Step (18 Counts)

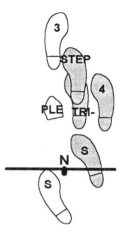

1-1   Right foot steps forward

1-&   Left foot steps forward

2-2   Right foot steps forward

3-3   Left foot steps forward

4-4   Right foot steps back

Left Triple Step, Step, Rock (5-8 Counts)

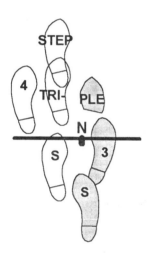

5-1   Left foot steps forward

5-&   Right foot steps forward

6-2   Left foot steps forward

7-3   Right foot steps back

8-4   Rock forward on left foot

Right Triple Step, Step, Pivot (9-12 Counts)

9-1   Right foot steps forward

9-&   Left foot steps forward

10-2   Right foot steps forward

11-3   Left foot steps forward

12-4   Pivot right 1/2 on left foot

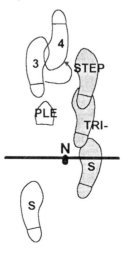

Left Triple Step, Step, Pivot (13-16 Counts)

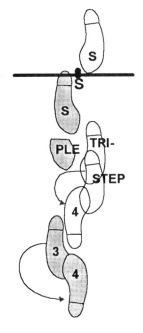

13-1   Left foot steps forward

13-&   Right foot steps forward

14-2   Left foot steps forward

15-3   Right foot steps forward

16-4   Pivot 1/2 left

Step, Turn (17-18 Counts)

17-1   Right foot steps forward

18-2   Turn 1/2 left on left

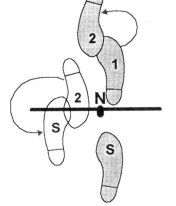

END — Le Doux Shuffle

TRASHY WOMEN

Line dance, easy advanced, 2 walls — 56 counts
Music: "Trashy Women" by Confederate Railroad
Description:

The song makes this a fun dance, which probably will withstand the test of time. The kicks and the Monterey turns add to the difficulty of the dance. The claps are optional, but they help you keep time and the rhythm.

Step, Slide, Step, Slide (1-4 Counts)

1-1   Left foot steps to left side

2-2   Right foot slides to left foot

3-3   Left foot steps to left side

4-4   Right foot slides to left foot — Clap

Step, Slide, Step, Slide (5-8 Counts)

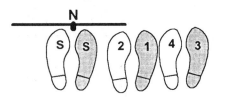

5-1   Right foot steps to right side

6-2   Left foot slides to right foot

7-3   Right foot steps to right side

8-4   Left foot slides to right foot — Clap

Jump Out, Cross, Turn, Clap (9-12 Counts)

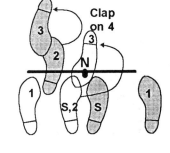

9-1   Both feet jump out

10-2   Both feet with right foot crossing in front of left

11-3   Turn left 1/2

12-4   Pause and clap

Right, Right, Left, Left (13-16 Counts)

13-1   Bounce hips right

14-2   Bounce hips right

15-3   Bounce hips left

16-4   Bounce hips left

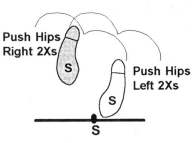

37-1 Right toe touches to right side

38-2 Turn 1/2 right on left foot, bringing right foot back by left

39-3 Left toe touches to left side

40-4 Close — Left foot back by right foot

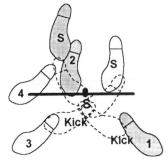

Swing Hips In Full Circle 2Xs

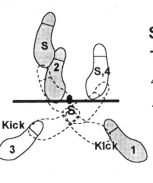

Step, Touch, Step, Touch, Step, Touch, Step, Touch (41-48 Counts)

41-1 Left foot steps back, 1/8 to the left

42-2 Right toe touches by left — Clap

43-3 Right foot steps back, 1/8 to the right

44-4 Left toe touches by right — Clap

45-5 Left foot steps back, 1/8 to the left

46-6 Right toe touches by left — Clap

47-4 Right foot steps back, 1/8 to the right

48-8 Left foots steps by right — Clap

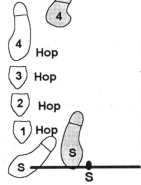

Left, Left, Right, Right (49-52 Counts)

49-1 Rock hips to left, then center

50-2 Rock hips to left

51-3 Rock hips to right, then center

52-4 Rock hips to right

Roll Hips 2Xs (53-56 Counts)

53-1&2 Roll hips in full circle — 2 counts

55-3&4 Roll hips in full circle — 2 counts

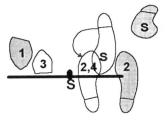

Monterey Spin (37-40 Counts)

37-1 Right toe touches to right side

38-2 Turn 1/2 right on left foot, bringing right foot back by left

39-3 Left toe touches to left side

40-4 Close — Left foot back by right foot

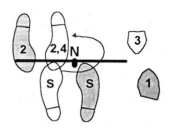

Step, Touch, Step, Touch, Step, Touch, Step, Touch (41-48 Counts)

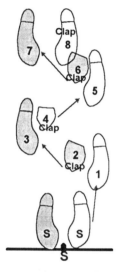

41-1 Left foot steps back, 1/8 to the left

42-2 Right toe touches by left — Clap

43-3 Right foot steps back, 1/8 to the right

44-4 Left toe touches by right — Clap

45-5 Left foot steps back, 1/8 to the left

46-6 Right toe touches by left — Clap

47-4 Right foot steps back, 1/8 to the right

48-8 Left foots steps by right — Clap

Left, Left, Right, Right (49-52 Counts)

49-1 Rock hips to left, then center

50-2 Rock hips to left

51-3 Rock hips to right, then center

52-4 Rock hips to right

Roll Hips 2Xs (53-56 Counts)

53-1&2 Roll hips in full circle — 2 counts

55-3&4 Roll hips in full circle — 2 counts

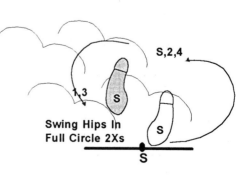

THE TUSH PUSH

Line dance, moderately easy, 4 walls — 40 counts

Music: "Super Love" by Exile, "Stand Up" by Mel McDaniel, "Hillbilly Rock" by Marty Stuart, "When Twist Comes to Shout" by Sawyer Brown, "Back Roads" by Ricky Van Shelton, "T-R-O-U-B-L-E" by Travis Tritt

Description: Very, very popular, fast moving line dance that everyone wants to do. The dance offers several opportunities for self expression. The turns are built around the CHA-CHA step.

Heel, Toe, Heel, Heel (1-4 Counts)

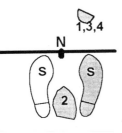

1-1	Right heel touches forward
2-2	Right toe touches by left heel
3-3	Right heel touches forward
4-4	Tap heel to floor again

Hop, Toe, Heel, Heel (5-8 Counts)

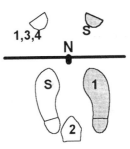

5-1   Hop, with left heel touching forward — Bring right foot back to center

6-2   Left toe touches by right heel

7-3   Left heel touches forward

8-4   Tap heel again

Hops (9-12 Counts)

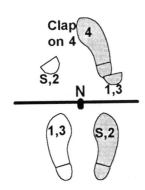

9-1	Hop — Left foot steps back and right heel touches forward
10-2	Hop — Right foot steps back and left heel touches forward
11-3	Hop — Left foot steps back and right heel touches forward
12-4	Pause and clap hands (shift weight to right foot)

Push Tush -- 2 To The Front & 2 To The Rear (13-16 Counts)

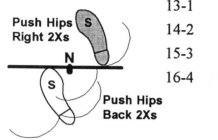

13-1   Rock hips forward

14-2   Rock hips forward

15-3   Rock hips back

16-4   Rock hips back

Push Tush -- Front, Rear, Front, Rear (17-20 Counts)

17-1   Rock hips forward

18-2   Rock hips back

19-3   Rock hips forward

20-4   Rock hips back

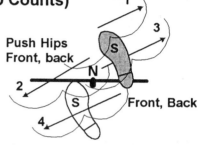

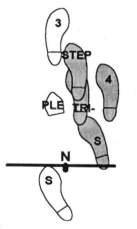

Triple Step Right, Step, Rock (21-24 Counts)

21-1   Right foot steps forward

21-&   Left foot steps forward

22-2   Right foot steps forward

23-3   Left foot steps forward — Shift weight to left foot

24-4   Right foot steps back

Triple Step Left, Step, Rock (25-28 Counts)

25-1   Left foot steps forward

25-&   Right foot steps forward

26-2   Left foot steps forward

27-3   Right foot steps back

28-4   Left foot rocks forward

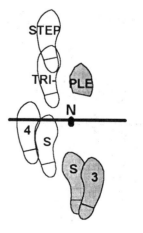

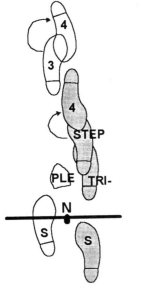

Triple Step Right, Step, Pivot (29-32 Counts)

29-1   Right foot steps forward

29-&   Left foot steps forward

30-2   Right foot steps forward

31-3   Left foot steps forward

32-4   Pivot right 1/2

Triple Step Left, Step, Pivot (33-36 Counts)

33-1   Left foot steps forward

33-&   Right foot steps forward

34-2   Left foot steps forward

35-3   Right foot steps forward

36-4   Pivot 1/2 left on right foot

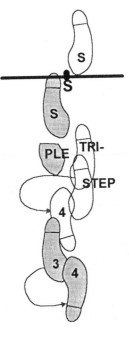

Step, Pivot, Close, Clap (37-40 Counts)

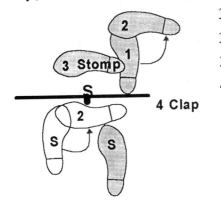

37-1   Right foot steps forward

38-2   Pivot 1/4 left on right foot

39-3   Close, right foot stomps by left

40-4   Clap hands

Chapter 8
Advanced Expert Line Dances

ACHY BREAKY

Line dance, moderately difficult, 4 walls — 32 counts

Choreography by Melanie Greenwood

Music: "Achy Breaky Heart" by Billy Ray Cyrus

Description: The stepping back turn makes the dance seem difficult. Some teachers will not even teach this dance because of the difficulty. The public interest in the ACHY BREAKY has faded, but the dance did a lot to generate the popularity of line dancing.

Some dances should only be performed to the music with which they were choreographed. This is one of those line dances.

Grapevine Right (1-4 Counts)

1-1   Right foot steps to right side

2-2   Left foot steps behind right

3-3   Right foot steps right

4-4   Left foot steps to right foot (optional stomp and clap)

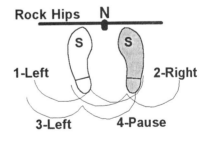

Swing Hips (5-8 Counts)

5-1   Swing hips to the left

6-2   Swing hips to the right

7-3   Swing hips to the left

8-4   Pause — No movement

Rock Hips

1-Left   2-Right

3-Left   4-Pause

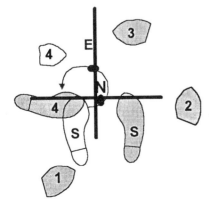

Touch, Touch, Turn, Turn (9-12 Counts)

9-1   Right toe touches behind left foot

10-2   Right toe touches right side

11-3   Right toe touches forward, turning 1/4 left

12-4   Turn left 1/2, end with weight on right foot

Step, Step, Hop, Step (13-16 Counts)

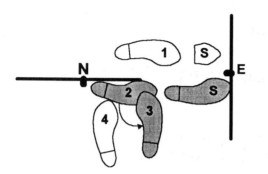

13-1 Left foot steps back

14-2 Right foot steps back

15-3 Hop on right foot, turning 1/4 left (lift left foot)

16-4 Step on left foot

Step, Step, Step, Stomp (17-20 Counts)

17-1 Right foot steps back

18-2 Left foot steps back

19-3 Right foot steps back

20-4 Stomp left foot and clap

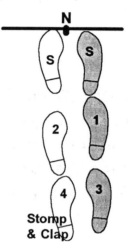

Swing Hips (21-24 Counts)

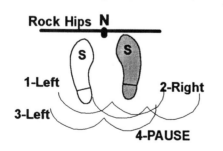

21-1 Swing hips left

22-2 Swing hips right

23-3 Swing hips left

24-4 Pause — No movement

Turn, Stomp, Turn, Stomp (25-28 Counts)

25-1   Right foot steps 1/4 right

26-2   Left foot stomps by right foot and clap

27-3   Left foot steps, 1/2 left

28-4   Right foot stomps by left and clap, turning 1/2 left

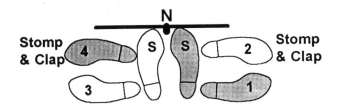

Grapevine Right, Stomp (29-32)

29-1   Right foot steps right

30-2   Left foot steps behind right foot

31-3   Right foot steps right

32-4   Left foot stomps by right foot and clap

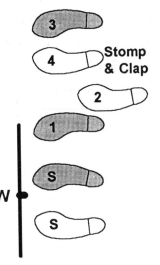

Note: The dance begins and ends with right grapevines, so don't let the back-to-back grapevines confuse you.

APPLE JACK

Line dance, advanced expert, 4 walls — 18 counts

Music: "Mercury Blues" by Alan Jackson, "Fireman" by George Strait

Description: The double time toe-heel swivels for the first eight counts make this dance difficult. There is continuous weight transfer on the swivels. With practice you can do it!

Left, Right (1-2 Counts)

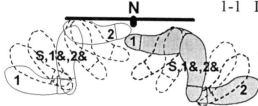

1-1 Left toe fans left (left heel remains in place), right heel swivels to center (right to remains in place)

1-& Close — Left and right heel move back to close position

2-2 Right toe fans right (right heel remains in place), left heel swivels to the center (left toe remains in place)

2-& Close — Move right toe and left heel to close position

Left, Left (3-4 Counts)

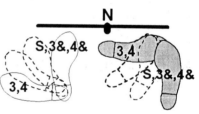

3-3 Left toe fans left (left heel remains in place), right heel swivels to center (right toe remains in place)

3-& Close — Left and right heel move back to close position

4-4 Left toe fans left (left heel remains in place), right heel swivels to center (right toe remains in place)

4-& Close — Left and right heel move back to close position

Right, Right (5-6 Counts)

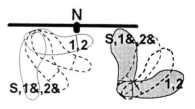

5-1 Right toe fans right (right heel remains in place), left heel swivels to the center (left toe remains in place)

5-& Close — Move right toe and left heel to close position

6-2 Right toe fans right (right heel remains in place), left heel swivels to the center (left toe remains in place)

6-& Close — Move right toe and left heel to close position

Left, Right (7-8 Counts)

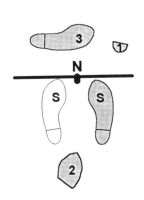

7-3 Left toe fans left (left heel remains in place), right heel swivels to center (right toe remains in place)

7-& Close — Left and right heel move back to close position

8-4 Right toe fans right (right heel remains in place), left heel swivels to the center (left toe remains in place)

8-& Close — Move right toe and left heel to close position

Heel, Toe, Turn, Toe (9-12 Counts)

9-1 Right heel touches forward

10-2 Right toe touches back by left heel

11-3 Right foot steps forward, turning 1/4 right

12-4 Left toe touches left

Step, Touch, Step, Step (13-16 Counts)

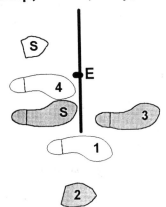

13-1 Left foot steps across (in front) right foot

14-2 Right toe touches right side

15-3 Right foot steps across (in front) left foot

16-4 Left foot steps back

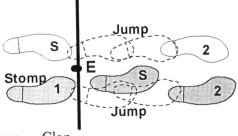

Close, Jump (17-18 Counts)

17-1 Close — Right foot stomps by left

18-2 Jump forward landing with feet together — Clap

COWBOY HIP HOP

Line dance, moderately difficult, 1 wall — 32 counts

Music: "Yippy-Ti-Yi-Yo" by Ronnie McDowell, "Yippy-Ti-Yi-Yo" by Kim Morrison/
Ronnie Godfrey, "Romeo" by Dolly Parton & Friends (same songs as HIP HOP)

Description: The COWBOY HIP HOP is an abbreviated version of the 96-step
THE HIP HOP, choreographed by Richard Tymko of Edmonton, Alberta. THE HIP
HOP is really a RAP or street dance. While jamming, a group of dancers in L.A. put
together a 168-count HIP HOP they called THE MAIN EVENT (HIP HOP). With
any of these HIP HOP dances, care should be exercised in properly warming up the
ankle and leg muscles. The COWBOY HIP HOP has been described by some
authorities as the "cutest" of the HIP HOPS.

Running Man (1-4 Counts)

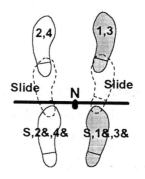

1-1   Right foot steps forward

1-&   Right foot slides back to close, lift left knee

2-2   Left foot steps forward

2-&   Left foot slides back to close, lift right knee

3-3   Right foot steps forward

3-&   Right foot slides back to close, lift left knee

4-4   Left foot steps forward

4-&   Left foot back to close, lift right knee

Hip Rolls (5-8 Counts)

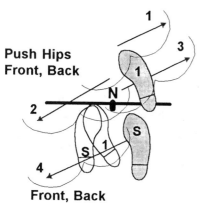

**Push Hips
Front, Back**

Front, Back

5-1   Right foot steps forward, pushing hips
       forward

6-2   Roll hips backward

7-3   Roll hips forward

8-4   Roll hips backward

Electric Kicks (9-12 Counts)

Note: left foot at same spot on the floor

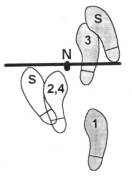

9-1   Right foot steps back

10-2   Left foot steps in place

11-3   Right foot steps forward

12-4   Left foot steps in place

Electric Kicks — Double Time (13-16 Counts)

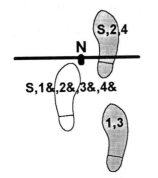

13-1   Right foot steps back, lift left foot

13-&   Left foot steps in place, lift right foot

14-2   Right foot steps forward, lift left foot

14-&   Left foot steps in place, lift right foot

15-3   Right foot steps back, lift left foot

15-&   Left foot steps in place, lift right foot

16-4   Right foot steps forward, lift left foot

16-&   Left foot steps in place

Grapevine Left, Stomp (17-20 Counts)

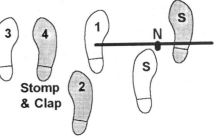

17-1   Left foot steps left

18-2   Right foot steps behind left

19-3   Left foot steps left

20-4   Right foot stomps by left and clap hands

Jump, Slide, Stomp, Stomp (21-24 Counts)

21-1   Jump to the right raising right knee, leaving left foot in place

22-2   Left foot drags to right, slowly

23-3   Left foot stomps

24-4   Right foot stomps

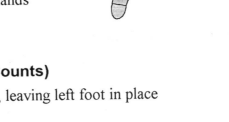

Jumping Jacks (25-28 Counts)

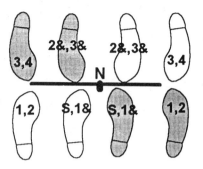

25-1   Jump, both feet apart

25-&   Jump, both feet together

26-2   Jump, both feet apart

26-&   Jump, right foot crosses in front of left, turning 1/2 left

27-3   Jump, both feet apart

27-&   Jump, both feet together

28-4   Jump, both feet apart

Frankensteins (29-32 Counts)

Note: Keep left leg stiff

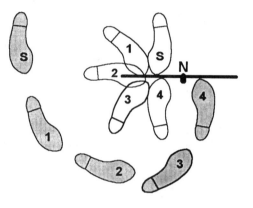

29-1   Right foot pushes, turning 1/8 left

30-2   Right foot pushes, turning 1/8 left

31-3   Right foot pushes, turning 1/8 left

32-4   Right foot pushes, turning 1/8 left

Note: With this dance there are many opportunities to add upper body styling. If the jumping jacks or hops physically bother you, feel free to replace them with buttermilks or swivels.

FOUR STAR BOOGIE

Line dance, advanced, 4 walls — 32 counts

Music: "I Feel Lucky" by Mary-Chapin Carpenter, "That's Country" by Marty Stuart

Choreographed by Melanie Greenwood

Description: One instructor describes the THE FOUR STAR BOOGIE as horrible to learn, but lots of fun after you learn it. The last four counts (hops) are the horrible part. You can do it!

Jump Forward, Jump Back (1-4 Counts)

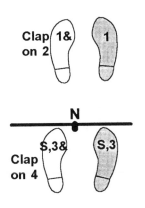

1-1	Jump forward, pushing off with left foot, right foot lands first
1-1&	Left foot lands by right foot
2-2	Hold — Clap
3-3	Jump back, pushing off with left foot, right foot lands first
3-3&	Left foot lands by right foot
4-4	Hold — Clap

Triple Step Right, Triple Step Left (5-8 Counts)

5-1   Right foot steps right

5-&   Left foot steps by right

6-2   Right foot steps right, turning 1/2 right

7-3   Left foot steps left

7-&   Right foot steps by left

8-4   Left foot steps left

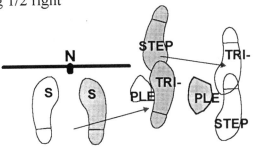

Triple Step 2Xs (9-12 Counts)

9-1   Right foot steps right

9-&   Left foot steps by right

10-2   Right foot steps right, turning 1/2 right

11-3   Left foot steps left

11-&   Right foot steps by left

12-4   Left foot steps left

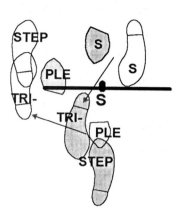

Vine Right (13-16 Counts)

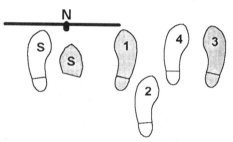

13-1   Right foot steps right

14-2   Left foot steps behind right

15-3   Right foot steps right

16-4   Left foot steps by right

Kick Ball Change (17-20 Counts)

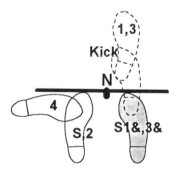

17-1   Right foot kicks forward

18-&   Right foot steps back

18-2   Left foot in place

19-3   Right foot kicks forward

19-&   Right foot steps back

20-4   Left foot steps in place, turning 1/4 right

Step, Kick Ball Change, Step (21-24 Counts)

21-1   Right foot steps right

22-2   Left foot kicks forward

22-&   Left foot steps by right

23-3   Right foot steps in place

24-4   Left foot steps in place — Clap

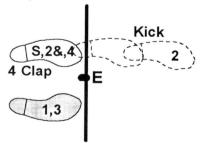

Triple Step, Step, Step (25-28 Counts)

25-1   Right foot steps forward

25-&   Left foot steps by right

26-2   Right foot steps forward

27-3   Left foot steps forward,
        turning 1/2 right

28-4   Right foot steps in place

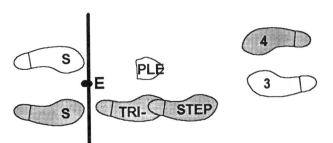

Star Jump (29-32 Counts)

29-1   Left toe points to left side

29-&   Left foot jumps to right foot

30-2   Right toe points to right side

30-&   Right foot jumps to left foot, turning 1/2 left

31-3   Left heel touches forward

31-&   Left foot jumps to right foot

32-4   Right toe points back

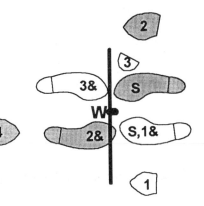

Note: On these last four counts, the center of gravity or center of movement remains in one place. Only the feet and legs move out.

To start over:

Jump Forward, Jump Back (1-4 Counts)

1-1   Right foot jumps forward, but push off with your left foot

1-&   Left foot lands by right foot

2-2   Hold — Clap

.... etc.

FUNKY COWBOY

Line Dance, advanced expert, 4 walls — 44 steps

Choreographed by Kevin Johnson and Vickie Vance

Music: "Funky Cowboy" by Ronnie McDowell, "Tulsa Time" by Don Williams

Description: FUNKY COWBOY has some different moves. Be patient with yourself and others while you are learning these new moves. Begin the dance on the 16th count of Funky Cowboy.

Note: Because of the knee moves, care should be taken with weak knees. Consult the proper medical authorities if necessary.

Dwight's — Knee Lifts (1-4 Counts)

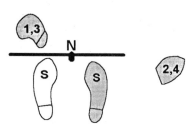

1-1   Right foot lifts to left knee as shoulders and body twist left

2-2   Right toe points to right side as shoulders and body twist right

3-3   Right foot lifts to left knee as shoulders and body twist left

4-4   Right toe points to right side as shoulders and body twist right

Heel Swings, Stomp (5-8 Counts)

Note: Keep right leg stiff for the first three counts.

5-5   Right heel touches in front of left foot as body and shoulders twist left

6-6   Right heel touches to right side as shoulders and body twist right

7-7   Right heel touches in front of left foot as body and shoulders twist left

8-8   Right foot stomps by left foot

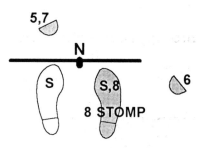

Roger Rabbit — Stomp, Turn, Drag, Step, Step, Step, Rock, Rock (9-16 counts)

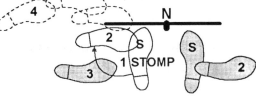

9-1   Left foot stomps by right

10-2   Right foot steps right, turning 1/4 right

11-3   Right foot drags back by left

12-4   Left foot swings (circles) left back

13-5   Left foot steps behind right foot

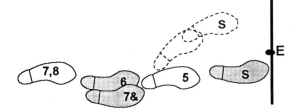

14-6   Right foot steps behind left

15-7   Left foot steps back

16-7& Right foot rocks forward

16-8   Left foot rocks back

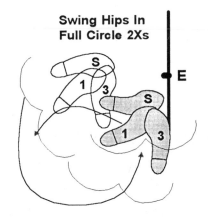

Swing Hips In Full Circle 2Xs

Two Hip Rolls (17- 20 Counts)

17-1   Roll hips right, turning left 1/8

18-2   Roll hips left

19-3   Roll hips right, turning left 1/8

20-4   Roll hips left

Stomp, Touch, Step, Touch, Hold (21-24 Counts)

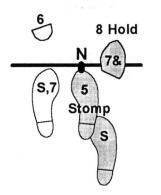

21-5   Right foot stomps by left

22-6   Left heel touches forward

23-7   Left foot steps back

23-7& Right toe touches forward, slightly

24-8   Hold — Right heel lifts off floor right knee bends (You are preparing for a right knee roll.)

Rubber Legs — Knee Rolls, Knee Bumps (25-32 Counts)

25-1   Right knee rolls out

26-2   Right knee rolls back

27-3   Left knee rolls out

28-4   Left knee rolls back

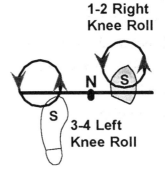

1-2 Right Knee Roll

3-4 Left Knee Roll

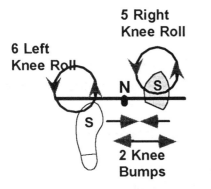

5 Right Knee Roll

6 Left Knee Roll

2 Knee Bumps

29-5   Right knee rolls out and back

30-6   Left knee rolls out and back

31-7   Knees bump together and both elbows out

31-7& Knees apart and both elbows down

32-8   Knees bump together and both elbows out

32-8& Knees apart and both elbows down

Note: Call out "Right, Left, Right, Left, Whoop, Whoop" as you do these movements.

Step, Slide, Turn, Touch, Step, Touch, Step, Touch (33-40 Counts)

33-1   Right foot steps right

34-2   Left foot slides right

35-3   Right foot steps right, turning 1/4 right

36-4   Left toe touches by right

37-5   Left foot steps left

38-6   Right toe touches by left

39-7   Right foot steps forward

40-8   Left toe touches by right foot

Out, Out, In, Cross — Pivot, Hold (41-44 Counts)

41-1 Left foot steps left — Out

41-1& Right foot steps right — Out

42-2 Left foot steps right — In

42-2& Right foot crosses over left

43-3 Turn left 1/2

44-4 Hold and clap

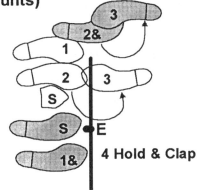

Hips Thrust, Body Wave (45-48 Counts)

45-5 Hips thrust forward and back, pulling outstretched fists to side

Note: Begin with both hands outstretched as if holding a set of barbells at waist height

46-6 Hips thrust forward and back, pulling outstretched fists to side

47-7 Body wave — First half

48-8 Body wave — Last half

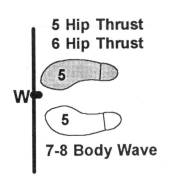

Note: A Body Wave is a two count move in which the whole body makes an upward rolling movement. The move begins with knees bent forward slightly, forcing the rear back. Begin with both fists outstretched at waist level in front. On the first count, the hips move forward, causing the shoulders to fall back. On the second count, the hips move from front to center and the shoulders move to their normal position. The fists move from front to your sides.

ROCKIN' ROBIN

Line dance, advanced, 2 walls — 48 counts

Music: "Honky Tonk Attitude" by Joe Diffie

Choreographer: Donna Wasnick

Description: Want a line dance that is a real challenge? If so, you'll love ROCKIN' ROBIN. Do you ever wonder where line dances get their names other than after the name of a song? Donna named ROCKIN' ROBIN after Robin, a red-haired member of the Tule Kicker Dance Club in Tulare, California. Have fun with the Monterey Turns.

Jazz Square Strut (1-8 Counts)

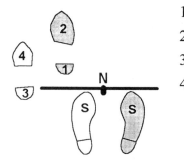

1-1   Cross — Right heel touches in front of left foot

2-2   Right toe steps down

3-3   Left heel touches back

4-4   Left toe steps down

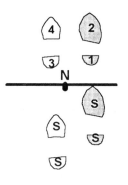

5-1   Right heel touches forward

6-2   Right toe steps down

7-3   Left heel touches by right foot

8-4   Left toe steps down

Heel, Heel, Toe, Toe (9-12 Counts)

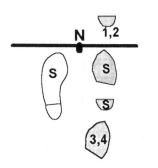

9-1   Right heel touches forward

10-2   Right heel touches forward

11-3   Right toe touches back

12-4   Right toe touches back

Heel, Slap, Heel, Slap (13-16 Counts)

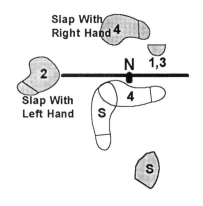

13-1   Right heel touches forward

14-2   Right foot lifts to left knee and slap boot with left hand

15-3   Right heel touches forward

16-4   Right foot swings to right side and slap boot with right hand while turning 1/4 left

Right, Behind, Right, In Front, Brush(17-20 Counts)

17-1   Right foot steps right

18-2   Left foot steps behind right

18-2&   Right foot steps right

19-3   Left foot steps in front of right

20-4   Right foot brushes left foot

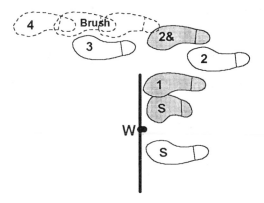

Cross Turns (21-24 Counts)

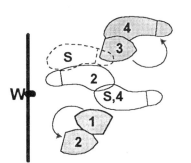

21-1   Right toe crosses left foot

22-2   Turn left 1/2 on toes

23-3   Right toe crosses left foot

24-4   Turn left 1/2 on toes

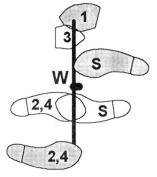

Monterey Spin 2Xs (25-32 Counts)

25-1   Right toe touches to right side

26-2   Right toe steps to center, while turning right 1/2

27-3   Left toe touches to left side

28-4   Close — Left foot steps by right foot

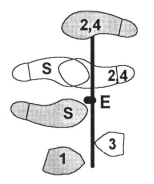

29-1 Right toe touches to right side

30-2 Right toe steps to center while turning right 1/2

31-3 Left toe touches to left side

32-4 Close — Left foot steps by right foot

Note: These Monterey Spins (Monterey Turns) are perhaps the most difficult part of the dance. Try saying "Step & Go, Step & No" for the step and turn, touch and close.

Rolling Left Turns (33-36 Counts)

33-1 Left foot steps forward, turning left 1/4

34-2 Right foot steps right, turning left 1/4

35-3 Left foot steps forward, turning left 3/4

36-4 Right foot stomps next to left

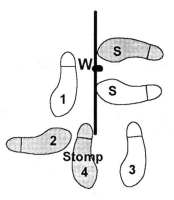

Toe Struts Back (37-40 Counts)

37-1 Right toe touches back

38-2 Right heel steps down

39-3 Left toe touches back

40-4 Left heel steps down

Hips Right, Hips Left (41-44Counts)

41-1   Right foot steps right, shifting weight to right hip

42-2   Right hip bumps right

43-3   Left hip bumps left, then back to center

44-4   Left hip bumps left, then back to center

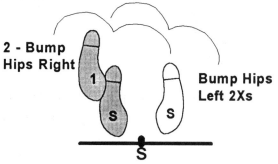

Hip Rolls (45-48 Counts)

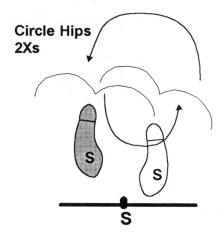

45-1   Roll hips right to left

46-2   Roll hips left to right

47-3   Roll hips right to left

48-4   Roll hips left to right

Note: The last four counts are just circling the hips two times.

TAKE IT EASY

Line dance, advanced expert, 2 walls — 48 counts

Music: "Take It Easy" by The Eagles, "Take It Easy" by Travis Tritt

Description: The cool move adds excitement to the dance, while the jump steps add difficulty.

Swivel, Turn (1-4 Counts)

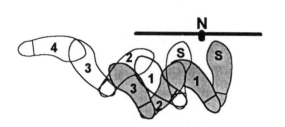

1-1	Swivel toes left
2-2	Swivel heels left
3-3	Swivel toes left
4-4	Left foot swivels 1/4 plus some right, right foot hitches — Right foot lifts

Step, Stomp, Turn, Stomp (5-8 Counts)

5-1 Right foot steps forward

6-2 Left foot stomps by right

7-3 Right foot steps forward, turning 1/4 left

8-2 Left foot stomps by right

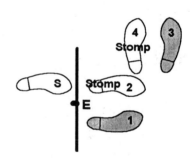

Right Turning Grapevine, Stomp (9-12 Counts)

9-1 Right foot steps right, turning 1/4 right

10-2 Left foot steps over right, turning 1/4 right

11-3 Right foot steps right, turning 1/2 right

12-4 Left foot stomps by right

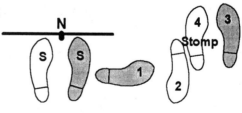

Kick Ball Change, Step, Touch (13-16 Counts)

13-1   Right foot kicks forward

14-2   Close — Right foot steps by left

14-&   Left foot steps in place

15-3   Right foot steps forward

16-4   Left toe touches by right

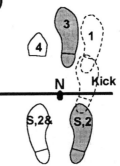

Step, Stomp, Turn, Brush (17-20 Counts)

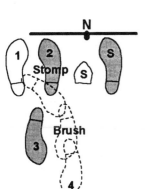

17-1   Left foot steps left

18-2   Right foot stomps by left

19-3   Right foot steps right, turning 1/2 right

20-4   Left foot brushes right

Grapevine Left, "Cool" (21-24 Counts)

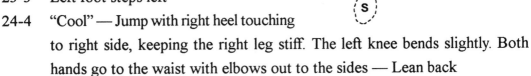

21-1   Left foot steps left

22-2   Right foot steps behind left

23-3   Left foot steps left

24-4   "Cool" — Jump with right heel touching

to right side, keeping the right leg stiff. The left knee bends slightly. Both hands go to the waist with elbows out to the sides — Lean back

Right Turning Grapevine, Stomp (25-28 Counts)

25-1 Right foot steps right, turning 1/4 right

26-2 Left foot steps over right, turning 1/4 right

27-3 Right foot steps right, turning 1/2 right

28-4 Left foot stomps by right

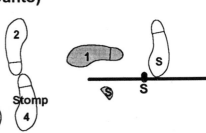

Step, Touch, Close, Stomp (29-32 Counts)

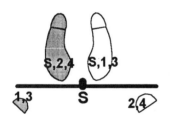

29-1 Left foot steps back

30-2 Right heel touches to the right side — Keep right leg stiff

31-3 Close — Right foot steps by left

32-4 Left foot stomps by right

Step, Touch, Close, Stomp (33-36 Counts)

33-1 Right foot steps back

34-2 Left heel touches to left side — Keep leg stiff

35-3 Close — Left foot steps by right

36-4 Right foot stomps by left

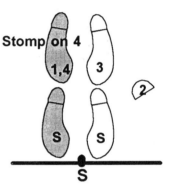

Cool Jumps (37-44 Counts)

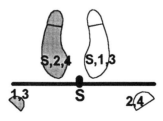

37-1 Right heel touches forward

38-2 Jump — Left heel touches forward, right foot back to close

39-3 Jump — Right heel touches forward, left foot back to close

40-4 Jump — Left heel touches forward, right foot back to close

41-1 Jump — Right heel touches forward, left foot back to close

42-2 Jump — Left heel touches forward, right foot back to close

43-3 Jump — Right heel touches forward, left foot back to close

44-4 Jump — Left heel touches forward, right foot back to close

Step, Scoot, Step, Stomp (45-48 Counts)

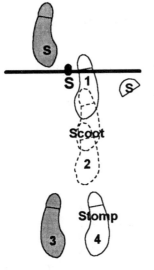

45-1   Left foot steps forward

46-2   Left foot scoots forward

47-3   Right foot steps forward

48-4   Left foot stomps by right

CHEROKEE KICK

Circle line dance, moderately easy — 36 counts

Music: "Cherokee Fiddle" by Johnny Lee

Note: The CHEROKEE KICK begins with dancers facing the center of the circle. The general direction of flow is counter-clockwise. With enough dancers, an inner circle can be formed. The dancers in the inside circle will face the dancers in the outside circle and move in the opposite direction.

Swivels (1-4 Counts)

1-1   Swivel heels right

2-2   Swivel heels to center

3-3   Swivel heels left

4-4   Swivel heels to center

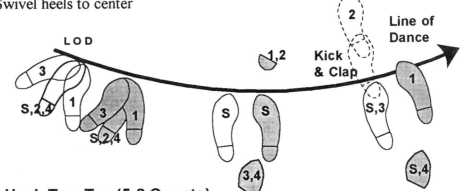

Heel, Heel, Toe, Toe (5-8 Counts)

5-1   Right heel touches forward

6-2   Right heel touches forward

7-3   Right toe touches back

8-4   Right toe touches back

Charleston (9-12 Counts)

9-1   Right foot steps forward

10-2   Left foot kicks forward and clap

11-3   Left foot steps back

12-4   Right toe touches back

Charleston (13-16 Counts)

13-1   Right foot steps forward

14-2   Left foot kicks forward and clap

15-3   Left foot steps left

16-4   Right toe touches back

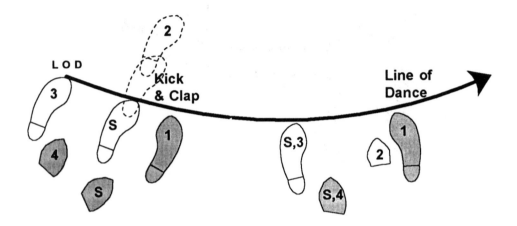

Step, Touch, Step, Touch (17-20 Counts)

17-1   Right foot steps right

18-2   Left toe touches by right

19-3   Left foot steps left

20-4   Right toe touches right

Grape Vine Right, Turn, Scoot (21-24 Counts)

21-1   Right foot steps right

22-2   Left foot steps behind right foot

23-3   Right foot steps right, turning 1/4 right

24-4   Right foot scoots forward

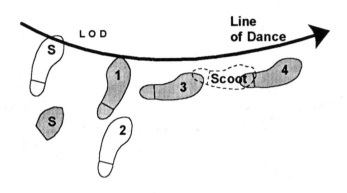

Turn, Scoot, Turn, Scoot (25-28 Counts)

25-1   Left foot steps, turning 1/2 right

26-2   Left foot scoots back

27-3   Right foot steps, turning 1/2 right

28-4   Right foot scoots forward

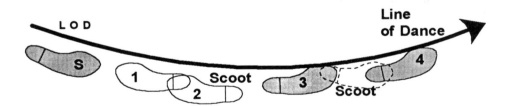

Walk, Walk, Scoot, Scoot (29-32 Counts)

29-1   Left foot walks forward

30-2   Right foot walks forward

31-3   Right foot scoots forward

32-4   Right foot scoots forward

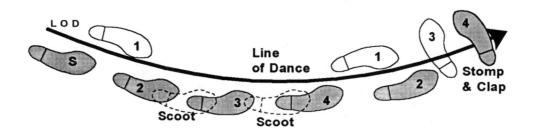

Walk, Walk, Turn, Stomp (33-36 Counts)

33-1   Left foot walks forward

34-2   Right foot walks forward

35-3   Left foot steps, turning 1/4 left

36-6   Right foot stomps by left and clap

MONTANA

Circle line dance, easy, 1 or 2 circles — 34 counts

Music: "Born to be Blue" by The Judds

Description: The dance begins with dancers forming a circle and facing the inside. With plenty of dancers, an inner circle can be formed as in CHEROKEE KICK.

Right Boot Hook (1-6 Counts)

1-1   Right heel touches forward

2-2   Close — Right toe touches by left

3-3   Right heel touches forward

4-4   Right heel lifts to left knee

5-5   Right heel touches forward

6-6   Close — Right foot steps by left

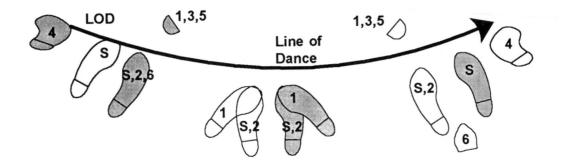

Buttermilk (7-8 Counts)

7-1   Spread heels out

8-2   Close — Heels together (say "Buttermilk" when heels are apart)

Left Boot Hook (9-14 Counts)

9-1   Left heel touches forward

10-2   Close — Left toe touches by right

11-3   Left heel touches forward

12-4   Left heel lifts to right knee

13-5   Left heel touches forward

14-6   Left toe touches by right heel

Charleston 2Xs (15-22 Counts)

15-1   Left foot steps forward

16-2   Right foot kicks forward and clap

17-3   Right foot steps back

18-4   Left toe touches back

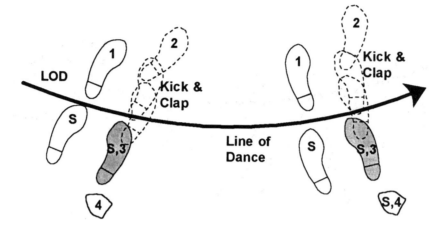

19-1   Left foot steps forward

20-2   Right foot kicks forward and clap

21-3   Right foot steps back

22-4   Left toe touches back

Vine Left (23-26 Counts)

23-1   Left foot steps left

24-2   Right foot steps behind left foot

25-3   Left foot steps left

26-4   Close — Right foot steps by left

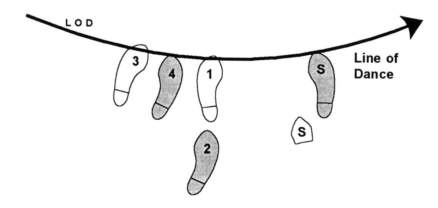

Vine Right, Pivot, Brush (27-30 Counts)

27-1   Right foot steps right

28-2   Left foot steps behind right

29-3   Right foot steps right, pivoting 1/2 right to outside of circle

30-4   Left foot brushes right foot

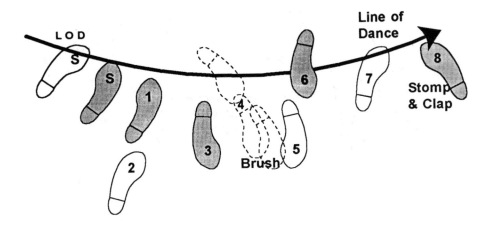

Vine Left, Pivot, Stomp (31-34 Counts)

31-5   Left foot steps left

32-6   Right foot steps behind left

33-7   Left foot steps left, pivoting 1/2 left to inside of circle

34-8   Right foot stomps and clap hands

ROULETTE WHEEL

Circle line dance, easy, 1 or 2 circles — 24 counts

Music: "Super Love" by Exile

Description: Start the dance facing the inside of the circle. The dance moves counter-clockwise. With enough dancers, an inner circle would move in the opposite direction — Clockwise. ROULETTE WHEEL and the other circle line dances are fun warm-up dances when a class starts. You get to see everyone in the class.

Vine Right And Turn, Vine Left And Turn (1-8 Counts)

1-1   Right foot steps right

2-2   Left foot steps behind right

3-3   Right foot steps right, turning 1/4 right

4-4   Right foot scoots, turning 1/4 right

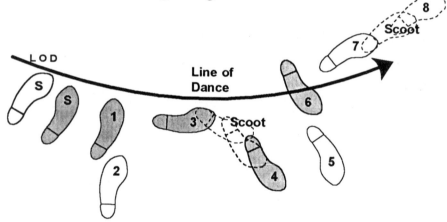

5-5   Left foot steps left

6-6   Right foot steps behind left

7-7   Left foot steps left, turning 1/4 left (facing line of dance)

8-8   Left foot scoots forward

Step, Bounce Hips Right, Left (9-12 Counts)

9-1   Right foot steps to outside of circle, bounce hips to right

10-2   Bounce hips to right

11-3   Bounce hips to left

12-4   Bounce hips to left

Bounce Hips Right, Left, Right, Left (13-16 Counts)

13-1 Bounce hips to right

14-2 Bounce hips to left

15-3 Bounce hips to right

16-4 Bounce hips to left

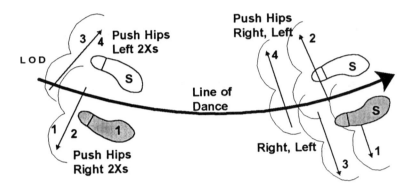

Bounce Hips Right, Left, Right, Left (17-20 Counts)

17-1 Right foot steps back, turning 1/4 right (turn to the outside with feet together)

18-2 Left toe touches forward

19-3 Left toe touches left side

20-4 Left toe touches back

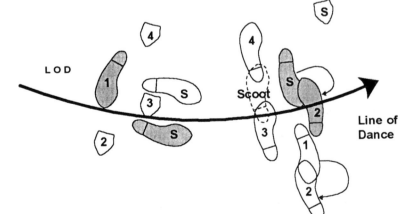

Step, Pivot, Step, Scoot (21-24 Counts)

21-1 Left foot steps forward

22-2 Left foot pivots, turning 1/2 right and facing inside of circle

23-3 Step on left foot

24-4 Left foot scoots forward (hitch), lift right foot — Clap hands

TRAVELING FOUR CORNERS

Circle line dance, easy, 1 or 2 circles — 20 counts

Music: "Cherokee Fiddle" by Johnny Lee, "Heartland" by George Strait, "I Love a Rainy Night" by Eddie Rabbit

Description: These circle dances are great as warm-up dances.

Heel Touches (1-5 Counts)

1-1   Left heel touches forward — Clap

2-2   Close — Left foot steps by right

3-3   Right heel touches forward — Clap

4-4   Close — Right foot steps by left

5-5   Left heel touches forward — Clap

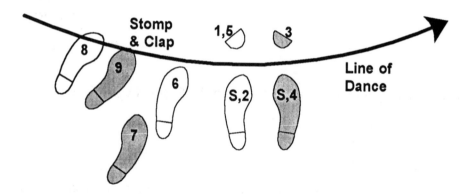

Grapevine Left, Turn (6-9 Counts)

6-6   Left foot steps left

7-7   Right foot steps behind left foot

8-8   Left foot steps left

9-9   Right foot stomps by left — Clap

Grapevine Right, Hop, Turn (10-13 Counts)

10-1   Right foot steps right

11-2   Left foot steps behind right foot

12-3   Right foot steps right

13-4   Right foot hops and turn 1/2 right, facing outside of circle — Clap

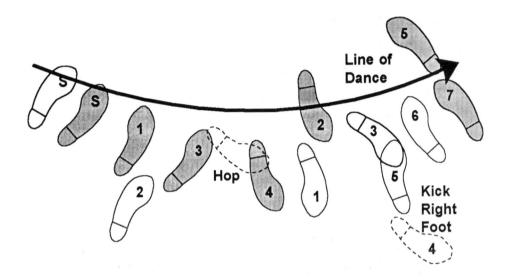

Grapevine Left, Swing Turn, Step, Rock, Step (14-20 Counts)

14-1   Left foot steps left

15-2   Right foot steps behind left foot

16-3   Left foot steps left

17-4   Left foot turns 1/2 left, kick — Swing right foot around, facing inside of circle — Clap

18-5   Right foot steps forward

19-6   Left foot rocks back

20-7   Right foot steps by left foot

Note: With two circles of dancers, it's fun to clap the hands of others on the hand claps.

Chapter 10
List of Dances and Music (Songs)

Dance	Type	Tempo	Song	Performer
1-STEP	Couples	150 BPM	Mirror Mirror	Diamond Rio
2-STEP	Couples	66 BPA 116 BPM 80 BPM 180 BPM 144 BPM	All My Exes Live in Texas City of New Orleans Come Early Morning Drive South Heartland If Your Heart Ain't Busy Tonight It's A Little Too Late Love's Got A Hold On You My Next Broken Heart Queen of Memphis	George Strait Willie Nelson Don Williams Suzy Bogguss George Strait Tanya Tucker Tanya Tucker R. Crowell / R. Cash Brooks and Dunn Confederate Railroad
3-STEP	Couples		It's Such A Small World	R. Crowell / R. Cash
6-COUNT SWING	Couples	176 BPM	T-R-O-U-B-L-E	Travis Tritt
6-STEP	Line	184 BPM	Norma Jean Riley	Diamond Rio
6 (COUNT) STEP	Line	184 BPM	Liza Jane	Vince Gill
8-COUNT *(Also known as HEY BARTENDER)*	Line		Hey Bartender	Johnny Lee
10-STEP *(Also known as THE TEXAS POLKA)*	Circle, Couples & Singles	 172 BPM	Devil Went Down To Georgia Eight Days A Week I Love A Rainy Night Orange Blossom Special Rocky Top The Fireman	Charlie Daniels Band Lorrie Morgan Eddie Rabbit Johnny Cash Roy Clark George Strait
14-STEP	Line	 196 BPM	Against The Grain Devil Went Down to Georgia I Love A Rainy Night Tennessee Flat Top Box	Garth Brooks Charlie Daniels Band Eddie Rabbit Rosanne Cash
16-STEP	Line	128 BPM	Bop	Dan Seals
ACHY BREAKY	Line	120/136 BPM	Achy Breaky Heart	Billy Ray Cyrus
ALLEY CAT	Line	120 BPM	Some Kind Of Trouble	Tayna Tucker

Dance	Type	Tempo	Song	Performer
APPLE JACK	Line	84 BPM 172 BPM	Mercury Blues The Fireman	Alan Jackson George Strait
ARIZONA 2-STEP	Couples		Any 2-STEP Music	
BARN DANCE	Couples Mixer	140 BPM	Don't Rock The Jukebox Dumas Walker Early In The Morning ...	Alan Jackson Kentucky Headhunters Wild Wild West
BLACKJACK	Line		I Love A Rainy Night Swinging Whiskey Ain't Workin' Anymore	Eddie Rabbit John Anderson Travis Tritt / Marty Stuart
BERRY JAM	Line	140 BPM 152 BPM	Hard Way To Make A Living Honky Tonk Attitude Queen Of Memphis	Bellamy Brothers Joe Diffie Confederate Railroad
BLACK VELVET	Line	94 BPM 92 BPM 112 BPM	Black Velvet No One Else On Earth She's Got The Rhythm Slow Hand Take It Back	Robin Lee Wynonna Judd Alan Jackson Conway Twitty Reba McEntire
BLUE MOON BOOGIE	Line		Born To Be Blue	The Judds
BOCEPHUS	Line	156 BPM 140 BPM	Boggie Cadillac Ranch Don't Call Him A Cowboy Forever And Ever Amen Hillbilly Rock There's A Tear In My Beer	Hank Williams Jr. Bruce Springsteen Conway Twitty Randy Travis Marty Stuart Hank Williams Jr.
BOOT SCOOTIN' BOOGIE	Line	132 BPM	Boot Scootin' Boogie I Am A Simple Man Risky Business	Brooks and Dunn George Strait Eddy Raven
CACTUS JACK ATTACK	Line		Any PONY SWING Music	
CADILLAC STYLE	Line	140 BPM	Cadillac Style	Sammy Kershaw
CHATTAHOOCHIE	Line	88 BPM	Chattahoochee River	Alan Jackson
CHEROKEE KICK	Line	80 BPM	Cherokee Fiddle Heartland	Johnny Lee George Strait
CHOCOLATE CITY HUSTLE	Line	128 BPM 140 BPM	Bop Dumas Walker Kansas City	Dan Seals Kentucky Headhunters Wilber Harrison

Dance	Type	Tempo	Song	Performer
CHOCOLATE CITY HUSTLE	Line	184 BPM	Norma Jean Riley	Diamond Rio
COPPERHEAD ROAD	Line	120 BPM 168 BPM 152 BPM 144 BPM	Achy Breaky Heart Bubba Shot The Jukebox Copperhead Road Queen Of Memphis Rock My Baby Tonight Wrong Side Of Memphis	Billy Ray Cyrus Mark Chesnutt Steve Earle Confederate Railroad Mighty Joe Young Trisha Yearwood
COTTON-EYED JOE	Couples	116 BPM	Cotton-Eyed Joe Someday Soon	Hank Williams Jr. Suzy Bogguss
COUNTRY STRUT	Line	128 BPM 120 BPM	Felicia Honky Tonk Blues Rap Top 'Round The Clock Lovin' She's An Old Cadillac Some Kind Of Trouble	McBride and The Ride Hank Williams Sr. Kentucky Headhunters K.T. Oslin Eddie Rabbit Tanya Tucker
COWBOY BOOGIE *(Also known as WATERGATE)*	Line	180 BPM 116 BPM 140 BPM 160 BPM	All My Rowdy Friends Born To Boogie Guitars, Cadillacs ... I Love A Rainy Night If I Said You Have A Beautiful Body My Next Broken Heart Redneck Girl Swingin' The Gulf Of Mexico Walk Of Life	Hank Williams Jr. Hank Williams Jr. Dwight Yoakam Eddie Rabbit Bellamy Brothers Brooks & Dunn Bellamy Brothers John Anderson Clint Black Dire Straits
COWBOY CHA-CHA	Couples & Line	128 BPM 88 BPM 100 BPM 106 BPM 116 BPM 108 BPM	Big Mexican Dinner Blue Days Grandpa Lovers Live Longer Our Love Tell Me I'm Only Dreamin'	Kentucky Headhunters Suzy Bogguss The Judds Bellamy Brothers Bellamy Brothers Lorrie Morgan
COWBOY HIP HOP *(Same songs as HIP HOP)*	Line	116 BPM 96 BPM	Romeo Yippy Ti Yi Yo Yippy Ti Yi Yo	Dolly Parton K. Morrison / R. Godfrey Ronnie McDowell
COWBOY HUSTLE		168 BPM 117 BPM 152 BPM 80 BPM	Bubba Shot The Jukebox Get Into Reggae, Cowboy Hard Workin'Man Heartland	Mark Chesnutt Bellamy Brothers Brooks & Dunn George Strait
COWBOY RHYTHM	Line	152 BPM	Hard Workin' Man	Brooks & Dunn

Dance	Type	Tempo	Song	Performer
COWGIRL DANCE	Line	112 BPM	Cowgirl Dance Don't Call Him A Cowboy Take It Back (S)	Ron Marshall Conway Twitty Reba McEntire
DUKE, THE	Line	80 BPM	Heartland	George Strait
EAST COAST SWING	Couples	148 BPM 132 BPM 168 BPM 164 BPM 220 BPM 176 BPM	Don't Rock The Jukebox Love Will Find Its Way To You Papa Loved Mama This Country's Rockin' This State Of Mind You Done Me Wrong	Alan Jackson Reba McEntire Garth Brooks The Judds Diamond Rio Trisha Yearwood
EIGHT CORNERS	Line	172 BPM	Hey Bartender The Fireman	Johnny Lee George Strait
ELECTRIC SLIDE	Line	128 BPM	Can't Touch This Electric Slide Pink Cadillac Put Some Drive In Your Country Stroking Turn It Loose Two Of A Kind/Workin' On A Full House Western Girls	M.C. Hammer M.C. Hammer Southern Pacific Travis Tritt Clarence Carter Doobie Brothers Garth Brooks Marty Stuart
ELVIRA CHA CHA	Line		Any Cha Cha Music	
ELVIRA	Line	66 BPM	All My Exes Live In Texas Elvira Elvira I Love A Rainy Night Why Not Me	George Strait Statler Brothers Oak Ridge Boys Eddie Rabbit The Judds
FLYING 8	Line	80 BPM	Cherokee Fiddle (S) Freeze Frame Heartland I Love A Rainy Night Linda On The Road Again	Johnny Lee J Giles Band George Strait Eddie Rabbit Steve Wariner Eddie Rabbit
FOUR STAR BOOGIE	Line	124 BPM 120 BPM	I Feel Lucky Now That's Country	Mary-Chapin Carpenter Marty Stuart
FREEZE FRAME	Line	80 BPM	Cherokee Fiddle Heartland	Johnny Lee George Strait
FREEZE	Line	124 BPM	Harper Valley PTA Stand Up Whiskey Ain't Workin' Anymore	Jeannie C Riley Mel McDaniel Travis Tritt

Dance	Type	Tempo	Song	Performer
FUNKY COWBOY	Line	120 BPM	Funky Cowboy Tulsa Time	Ronnie McDowell Don Williams
GET RHYTHM	Line	220 BPM 120 BPM	Get Rhythm Get Rhythm Some Kind Of Trouble	Norton Del Ray Johnny Cash Tayna Tucker
GOLD COAST	Line	128 BPM 100 BPM	Pink Cadillac Risky Business Walkin' After Midnight	Southern Pacific Eddy Raven Garth Brooks
HAWAIIAN	Line	66 BPM	All My Exes Live In Texas	George Strait
HUSTLE		 116 BPM	Early In The Morning, Late At Night Earthquake I Am A Simple Man Put Some Drive In Your Country Rockin' To The Rhythm Of The Rain Romeo	Hank Williams Jr. Ronnie Milsap George Strait Travis Tritt The Judds Dolly Parton
HILLBILLY ROCK HIP HOP	Line Line	140 BPM	Hillbilly Rock Bust A Move Pump Up The Jam Vogue	Marty Stuart M.C. Young Kamosi-De-Quincey Madonna
HONKY TONK STOMP	Line		Watch Me	Lorrie Morgan
HONKY TONK WALKIN'	Line	120 BPM	Honky Tonk Walkin'	Kentucky Headhunters
HORSESHOE	Couples	 112 BPM	Learning How To Live She Don't Know She's Beautiful	Garth Brooks Sammy Kershaw
HUSTLE (COWBOY SHUFFLE)	Line		Rockin' To The Rhythm ...	The Judds
J WALK	Couples & Line		Mississippi Take One Heart Beat At A Time	Charlie Daniels Band Oak Ridge Boys
JASON	Line		Lonesome Me	Kentucky Headhunters
JUG COUNTRY	Line	124 BPM	I Feel Lucky	Mary-Chapin Carpenter
LA WALK	Line		Baby's Got Her Blue Jeans On Somewhere Tonight There's A Tear In My Beer Walk This Way	Mel McDaniel Highway 101 Hank Williams Jr. Hank Williams Jr.

Dance	Type	Tempo	Song	Performer
LE DOUX SHUFFLE	Line	156 BPM	Cadillac Ranch I Love A Rainy Night Western Girls	Chris LeDoux Eddie Rabbit Marty Stuart
LONE STAR	Line	126 BPM	I Love A Rainy Night Rockin' To The Rhythm Of The Rain Why Not Me	Eddie Rabbit The Judds The Judds
LUCKY	Line	124 BPM	I Feel Lucky	Mary-Chapin Carpenter
MONTANA	Couples & Line		Born To Be Blue	The Judds
NEON MOON	Line	104 BPM 108 BPM	Any CHA-CHA Music Neon Moon Cross My Broken Heart	Brooks & Dunn Suzy Bogguss
PASADENA POLKA	Line & Couples	116 BPM 140 BPM 132 BPM	Next Thing Smokin' This Night Life Whatcha Gonna Do	Joe Diffie Clint Black Chris LeDoux
PONY SWING	Couples	232 BPM 188 BPM 208 BPM	Do I Ever Cross Your Mind Heart of Hearts Let Me Tell You About Love	Randy Travis Randy Travis The Judds
REDNECK GIRL	Line	160 BPM 160 BPM	Redneck Girl Redneck Girl	Bellamy Brothers Kentucky Headhunters
REGGAE COWBOY	Line	117 BPM	Get Into Reggae Cowboy	Bellamy Brothers
RENEGADE SCHOTTISCHE	Couples & Mixer		Rockin' To The Rhythm Of The Rain	The Judds
RIDIN' DOUBLE	Couples	160 BPM	Redneck Girl	Bellamy Brothers
ROCKABILLY BOGGIE	Line	128 BPM 140 BPM 136 BPM	Bop Don't Call Him A Cowboy Hillbilly Rock I'm A One Man Woman One Step Forward Walk This Way	Dan Seals Conway Twitty Marty Stuart The Judds Desert Rose Band Hank Williams Jr.
ROCKIN' ROBIN	Line	140 BPM	Honky Tonk Attitude	Joe Diffie
ROLLING STONE	Line	120 BPM 122 BPM	Honky Tonk Walkin' Hooked On a 10-Second Ride Men Rolling Stone	Kentucky Headhunters Chris LeDoux The Forester Sisters Larry Dean

Dance	Type	Tempo	Song	Performer
ROLLING STONE		176 BPM	Shake The Sugar Tree When Did You Stop Loving Me	Pam Tillis George Strait
ROULETTE WHEEL (GC)	Line		Super Love Turn It Loose	Exile Doobie Brothers
RUM PUNCH	Line		Kiss Me In The Car	John Berry
SAGE BRUSH	Line		Chase Each Other 'Round The Room Mama's Never Seen Those Eyes Somewhere Tonight There's A Tear In My Beer	Merle Haggard The Forester Sisters Highway 101 Hank Williams Sr.
SCHOTTISCHE	Couples	156 BPM 116 BPM 120 BPM	Dallas I Am A Simple Man Seminole Winds (S) Turn It Loose	Alan Jackson Ricky Van Shelton John Anderson The Judds
SHOTGUN	Line	140 BPM	Diggin' Up Bones Hillbilly Rock Mama's Never Seen Those Eyes	Randy Travis Marty Stuart The Forester Sisters
SKI BUMPUS	Line	116 BPM 122 BPM	Chains I Am A Simple Man I'm Over You Men	Patty Loveless Ricky Van Shelton Keith Whitley The Forester Sisters
SLAPPIN' LEATHER	Line	164 BPM 140 BPM 140 BPM 172 BPM 176 BPM	Back Roads Have Mercy Hillbilly Rock Little Sister Some Girls Do Stand Up The Fireman T-R-O-U-B-L-E You Can't Keep A Good Man Down	Ricky Van Shelton The Judds Marty Stuart Dwight Yoakum Sawyer Brown Mel McDaniel George Strait Travis Tritt Wynonna Judd
SLEAZY SLIDE	Line	120 BPM	I Feel Lucky The Sleazy Slide	Mary Chapin Carpenter Pat Garrett
SLEEZE, THE	Line	128 BPM	Bop	Dan Seals
SLIDIN' HOME	Line	128 BPM 120 BPM	If It Wasn't For Her I Wouldn't Have You Kiss Me In The Car	Daron Norwood John Berry
SLO CADILLAC	Line	128 BPM	Baby I'm Yours Blue To The Bone Bop I'm So Lonesome	Steve Wariner Sweethearts Of The Rodeo Dan Seals Hank Williams Jr.

Dance	Type	Tempo	Song	Performer
SLO CADILLAC			Pink Cadillac Somewhere Tonight	Bruce Springsteen Highway 101
SNOWBIRD SHUFFLE	Line	138 BPM	Jealous Bone	Patty Loveless
SOUTH SIDE SHUFFLE	Line	164 BPM 140 BPM	Back Roads Hillbilly Rock Stand Up Super Love When Twist Comes To Shout	Ricky Van Shelton Marty Stuart Mel McDaniel Exile Sawyer Brown
SPLIT RAIL	Line	128 BPM	Bop Don't Call Him A Cowboy Linda Mama's Never Seen Those Eyes	Dan Seals Conway Twitty Steve Wariner The Forester Sisters
STRAY CAT STRUT	Line	150 BPM 92 BPM	Mirror Mirror She's Got the Rhythm Stray Cat Strut	Diamond Rio Alan Jackson Stray Cats
STROKING	Line		Stroking	Clarence Carter
SUGAR TREE	Line		Shake The Sugar Tree	Pam Tillis
T. C. ELECTRIC SLIDE	Line	124 BPM 128 BPM 120 BPM	Born To Be Blue Electric Slide I Feel Lucky Pink Cadillac Some Kind of Trouble Stroking The Radio	Sweethearts Of The Rodeo H.C. Hammer Mary-Chapin Carpenter Southern Pacific Tanya Tucker Clarence Carter Vince Gill
TAHOE TWIST	Line	172 BPM	18 Wheels And A Dozen Roses Headed for a Heartache T for Texas The Fireman Two More Bottles of Wine	Kathy Mattea Gary Morrris Waylon Jennings George Strait Emmylou Harris
TAKE IT EASY	Line	140 BPM	Take It Easy Take It Easy	The Eagles Travis Tritt
TENNESSEE TWISTER	Line	112 BPM 120 BPM	Take It Back What Part Of No ... Wild Man	Reba McEntire Lorrie Morgan Ricky Van Shelton
TEXAS COUNTY LINE	Line	108 BPM 100 BPM 116 BPM 104 BPM	Any CHA-CHA Music Cross My Broken Heart Grandpa If I Said You Had A Beautiful Body Neon Moon	Suzy Bogguss The Judds Bellamy Brothers Brooks & Dunn

Dance	Type	Tempo	Song	Performer
TEXAS SCHOTTISCHE	Couples	112 BPM	I'm A One Man Woman	The Judds
TRASHY WOMEN	Line	144 BPM	Trashy Women	Confederate Railroad
TRAVELING FOUR CORNERS (GC&C)	Couples & Line	80 BPM	Cherokee Fiddle Heartland I Love A Rainy Night	Johnny Lee George Strait Eddie Rabbit
TULSA TIME	Line	124 BPM	Tulsa Time Tulsa Time	Don Williams Pat Garrett
TULSA TIME II	Line	120 BPM 136 BPM 124 BPM	Achy Breaky Heart One Step Forward Tulsa Time	Billy Ray Cyrus Desert Rose Band Pat Garrett
TUSH PUSH	Line	164 BPM 180 BPM 140 BPM 140 BPM 176 BPM 164 BPM	Back Roads Born To Boogie Dumas Walker Hillbilly Rock Stand Up Super Love T-R-0-U-B-L-E When Twist Comes To Shout	Ricky Van Shelton Hank Williams Jr. Kentucky Headhunters Marty Stuart Mel McDaniel Exile Travis Tritt Sawyer Brown
WANDERER	Line	120 BPM	Have Mercy The Wanderer	The Judds Eddie Rabbitt
WALKIN' WAZIE	Line	88 BPM 140 BPM	Chattahoochee River Crime Of Passion Dumas Walker I'm Gonna Get You Stand Up Tear Stained Letter We'll Burn That Bridge Western Girls	Alan Jackson Ricky Van Shelton Kentucky Headhunters Eddy Raven Mel McDaniel Jo-El Sonnier Brooks & Dunn Marty Stuart
WALTZ	Couples & Line	101 BPM 112 BPM 116 BPM	Famous Last Words Of A Fool Here's A Quarter Something In Red Tennessee Waltz You Look So Good In Love Warning Labels	George Strait Travis Tritt Lorrie Morgan Lacy J. Dalton George Strait Doug Stone

Dance	Type	Tempo	Song	Performer
WALTZ ACROSS TEXAS	Line	96 BPM 100 BPM	Any WALTZ Music Here's A Quarter High Lonesome Last Cheaters Waltz Something In Red Tennessee Waltz Waltz Across Texas You Look So Good In Love	Travis Tritt Randy Travis Emmylou Harris Lorrie Morgan Lacy J. Dalton Willie Nelson George Strait
WALTZ MIXER	Couples		Any WALTZ Music	
WEST COAST SWING	Couples	112 BPM 140 BPM 156 BPM 120 BPM 128 BPM 92 BPM	Hand Over Your Heart Hillbilly Rock Nobody's Fool Some Kind Of Trouble You Really Had Me Going Wherever You Are	Lorrie Morgan Marty Stuart McBride & The Ride Tanya Tucker Holly Dunn Highway 101
WESTERN GIRLS	Line	128 BPM	Any Slow SWING Music Western Girls	Marty Stuart
WESTERN SLIDE	Line	128 BPM	Pink Cadillac Pump Up The Jam Turn It Loose	Southern Pacific Kamosi-De-Quincey Doobie Brothers
WILD SLIDE	Line	120 BPM	Wild Man	Ricky Van Shelton
WILD WILD WEST	Line		Any Fast CHA-CHA Music I Had A Beautiful Time Wild Wild West	Merle Haggard Escape Club
WHISKEY RIVER	Line		Born To Be Blue Whiskey River Whiskey River	The Judds Willie Nelson The Judds

Ball And Change—A ball and change is a step on the ball of one foot followed by a quick change of weight to the other foot. It usually is done as part of a kick ball change *(See Kick Ball Change)*.

Beat—The beat is any of a series of sounds that make up music. Thus, the beat is the unit of musical rhythm.

Brush—A brush is a sweeping, kissing or scuffing movement of one foot against the floor, while the other supports your body weight.

Buttermilk—A buttermilk (aka: butterfly, heel splits, splits, scissors, pigeon toes) is the dance movement performed by rising up onto the toes of both feet and spreading the heels apart, then bringing the heels back together. Each buttermilk takes two counts.

Cha-Cha—The CHA-CHA is a Latin dance step with two parts: a forward half and a back half — 10 steps performed in 8 counts. Each half has 2 steps, followed by a triple step (shuffle step — 2 counts).

Charleston / Charleston Step—A Charleston or Charleston step is a 3- or 4-count step pattern. For example, in a right Charleston, you step forward on the left foot, kick forward with the right foot, step back on the right foot, and then touch your left foot behind your right foot.

Clap—A clap is the act of striking the palms of two hands together. The hands do not necessarily have to be attached to the same body.

Close / Close Position—Close is the position in which both feet are together under the center of the body, heels together and toes together. Professional dancers refer to the close position as the first position—neutral or parallel.

Count / Counting—Counting can be defined as keeping time with the music by counting the beats. A whole or full count is one beat, also a measure of time. Generally, you take one step or movement for each count or beat. A half beat or half count (the *and* count is half of a whole count) is twice as fast as a whole count.

Cross / Crossover Left, Crossover Right—One foot moving in front of the other is referred to as a cross or cross step.

Duck Walk—The duck walk (aka: strut or country strut) is a 2-count step in which you touch the heel to the floor, then roll the toes or slap them to the floor.

Fan—A fan is the swinging of the foot, with the heel as the pivotal point. The toes swing from the front to the side, and back to the front again.

Grapevine / Vine — A grapevine (aka: grapevine right, grapevine left, vine right, vine left) is a 3- or 4-count series of steps. You step to the side with one foot, step behind with the other foot, and step to the side again with the first foot. The last foot move (count) can be a stomp, brush, touch, step or scoot.

Hip Bumps—Rocking the hips to one side is referred to as hip bumps. The hips are rocked by keeping one knee stiff and bending the opposite knee.

Heel—A heel refers to the heel of the foot touching the floor, usually in front of the body.

Hitch—A hitch is the lifting of the leg at the knee, generally while scooting or hopping.

Hold / Pause / Rest—Remaining in the last position with no movement is referred to as a hold, pause or rest.

Hook / Boot Hook—The hook (aka: boot hook, right hook, left hook, right boot hook, left boot hook) is a 4-count series of movements in which the heel touches forward, the heel is lifted to the opposite knee, the heel touches forward, close. The hook can be done with the right or left foot. Depending upon the accent of the boot hook, the heel will lift toward the knee. With a full boot hook, the calf of the leg will touch just below the knee cap.

Hop—A hop is the leap or spring of the body forward, backward or sideways without changing body weight to the other foot. The hop differs from a scoot in that with a hop, the foot or feet leave the floor. With a scoot, the foot or feet remain in contact with the floor *(See Scoot)*.

Jazz Box / Jazz Square—The jazz box is a 3- or 4-count series of steps in which one foot crosses over the other, you step back with the opposite foot, and the first foot closes.

Jump—A jump is leaping upward and then landing on both feet.

Kick—A kick is the forward movement of either foot into the air.

Kick Ball Change—A kick ball change is a form of ball change. For example, the right foot is kicked forward, the right foot is brought back under the body and you step on the right foot, then change weight to the left foot. This is a 2-count movement.

Line of Dance / LOD—The line of dance refers to an imaginary, counterclockwise line on the outer three feet of the dance floor. Dancers use the line of dance to keep from bumping into each other. By convention, for country western dancing the line of dance is counterclockwise. It is interesting to note that line of dance follows the rules of the road for autos.

Monterey Spin—The Monterey spin is a 4-count half (180^0) turn in which you touch the right toe to the right side, turn one half to the right on the left foot, bring the right foot to the left foot, touch the left toe to the left side, step with the left foot by the right foot. A spin is a full or complete (360^0) turn. Thus, a Monterey spin is not a true spin.

Prance—The prance is a 4-count, full-body movement performed in place with the feet in close position. The knees swing left and right as they are bent to lower the body on the first two counts. On the third and forth counts, the processes are reversed. The arms are bent at the elbows to emphasize or accentuate the rocking motion. Shift weight with each swing and the feet may step in place on each count.

Point—A point (aka: point right, point left, point front, or point back) is a toe touch to the front, back or side with the body weight supported by the non-pointing foot.

Rhythm—Rhythm is the grouping of sounds in a piece of music. Musicians use musical instruments to produce rhythm (music) by the grouping of pulsations or beats.

Rock—A rock is a shifting of body weight from one foot to the other. The feet usually do not change position on the floor.

Scoot—A scoot is the forward movement of one foot while the other foot is lifted (hitched) off the floor. The scoot differs from the hop in that with a scoot, the scooting foot remains in contact with the floor.

Shimmy—A shimmy is the rapid shaking or shrugging of the shoulders by moving one shoulder forward and the other backward, then reversing the process.

Shuffle Step—(aka: shuffle step, right shuffle step, left shuffle step, triple step right, triple step left) *(See Triple Step)*

Slide—A slide is a foot movement along the floor in which the moving (drawing) foot remains in contact with the floor. Usually, one foot slides along the floor to the other foot.

Spin—A spin is a full, 360^0 turn performed on one foot.

Star—A star is a series of foot movements (points) in which the toe is pointed to the front, to the side, then to the rear (back).

Step—A step (aka: step right, step left, step forward, step back) is the act of moving by placing a foot in a different position and shifting body weight to that foot, usually executed on the beat. A step differs from a touch in that body weight is shifted from one foot to the other. With a touch, there is no shifting of body weight.

Stomp—A stomp is the striking of the whole foot on the floor, usually in an attempt to make loud noise.

Swivel—A swivel is the rotation on the balls of both feet from the center (close position) to one side or from the side back to center. A swivel is one half of a twist.

Tempo—Tempo is the pace or speed in which a piece is performed -- beats per minute (BPM). Tempo is the time between beats. Or, tempo is the distance between beats, measured in time.

Toe / Touch—A touch is when the foot touches the floor without a shifting of body weight. The heel or toe can touch the floor in front. The toe can touch the floor to the side or back.

Triple Step—The triple step or shuffle (aka: cha-cha, double step, polka step, triple rhythm step, shuffle, triple step, shuffle step, right shuffle step, left shuffle step, triple step right, triple step left) is three quick steps performed in two counts (counted as *1 - and - 2*) traveling in any direction. In the left forward shuffle step, you step forward with the left foot, step with the right toe to the left heel, and step forward with the left foot. You can do a forward or backward shuffle step.

Turn—A turn is the circular motion or change of direction that occurs when taking one or more steps.

Twist—A twist is the rotation on the balls of both feet from one side to the other side. A twist is two swivels.

Vine—*(See Grapevine)*

Wall—A wall refers to the direction of a line dance. There are four walls. A line dance will either be a 1-, 2- or 4-wall dance.

Weight Change—Weight change is the shift of body weight from one foot to the other.

REFERENCES

1. T. Beard, *The Cowboy Boot Book*, (Gibbs Smith, Publishers, Layton, Utah, 1992)

2. California Country Calendar, P.O. Box 3178, Walnut Creek, CA 94598.

3. R. Cohan, *The Dance Workshop*, (Simon & Schuster, Inc., New York, 1986).

4. Country Dance Lines, Drawer 139, Woodacre, CA 94973-0139.

5. R.W. Fanus, *Central Coast Country Western Dancin'* (Fanus Publishing, Lancaster, Calif., 1988).

6. K. Gellette, *Kelly Gellette's Country Western*, Kelly Gellette Vol I (Las Vegas, Nev., 1983).

7. K. Gellette, *Kelly Gellette's Country Western Hot Line Dances*, Kelly Gellette Vol XI (Las Vegas, Nev., 1993).

8. K. Gellette, *The line Dance, Partner Dance and Mixer Dance Book*, National Teachers Association for Country Western Dance (Las Vegas, Nev., 1993).

9. K. Gellette, *Kelly Gellette's Country Western Line Dances Galore*, Kelly Gellette Vol V (Las Vegas, Nev., 1988).

10. G. Giorodano, *Jazz Dance Class* (Princeton Book Company, Pennington, N.J., 1992).

11. D.K. Norris & Reva Shiner, *Keynotes to Modern Dance*, 2nd ed. (Burgess Publishing Co., Minneapolis, Minn., 1966).

12. J. Snyder & R. Higgins, *Comprehensive Guitar Method*, (Belwin Miles Publishing Corp., 1971).

13. P. Spencer, *Ballroom Dancing*, (NTC Publishing Group, Lincolnwood, Ill., 1992).

14. R.M. Stephenson & J. Iaccarino, *Complete Book of Ballroom Dancing*, (Boubleday, N.Y., N.Y., 1980).

15. L.M. Vincent, M.D., *The Dancer's Book of Health*, (Princeton Book Company, Pennington, N.J., 1988).

16. J. Woolman, *The New Country Western Line Dancer's Reference Handbook*, (Wild And Wooly Publications, Descanso, Calif, 1993)

17. J. Wright, *Social Dance Steps to Success*, (Leisure Press, Champaign, Ill., 1992).

Index

HILTON OSBORNE's
Run To The Floor For Country Western
LINE DANCING
Can be ordered direct !
Copies are only $19.95
plus $3.95 for Shipping and Handling
Include 8.25% Sales Tax for California Shipment

Yes Hilton, I need _____ copies for my friends.
Rush my order to :

Name :_____

Address :_____

City :_____

State :_____ Zip:_____

Phone :(_____)_____

QTY	AUTHOR / TITLE / ISBN	UNIT	
	Hilton Osborne Line Dancing ISBN: 1-882180-37-2	$19.95	A}
	State Sales Tax	8.25%	B}
	Shipping & Handling per Book	$3.95	C}
	Total of your Order { A x B + C }		

Type Payment: ☐ Check ☐ Credit Card ☐ Money Order

M / V: _____

EXP. DATE: ____ / ____ / _____
Send your Order to:
Griffin Publishing Dept. D500
544 W. Colorado Street
Glendale, California 91204

Can't Wait ?
Call in your Credit Card Order
1 {800} 423-5789 ext. 750
Fax 818 242-1172